chapel chats
for children
(of all ages)

Christian Education preschool & kindergarten

Jerald R. Borgie

XUlon
PRESS

RBCPC
17010 Pomerado Rd
San Diego, CA 92128

Chapel Chats for Children (of all ages)
Christian Education preschool & kindergarten
by Jerald R. Borgie

Printed in the United States of America

ISBN 9781629525310

www.xulonpress.com

Dedicated to my grandchildren
Andrew, Emma, Jonathan, Finley, and Luke

"I have no greater joy than to hear that my children
are walking in the truth." 3 John 4 (TNIV)

ACKNOWLEDGEMENTS

Thanks to two thousand preschoolers who over the past twenty years loved and were loved by Jesus, Jeremiah, and me; to Brooke Plowman, who first met Jeremiah as a preschooler and now as a professional artist provided marvelous illustrations for the book; to Nancy Clements, a long time neighbor and friend for many hours of proofreading; to Marcia, my cherished partner of forty-five years for her typing skills, encouragement and love.

TABLE OF CONTENTS

SPECIAL OCCASIONS

FORWARD

For over twenty years, Jeremiah, my koala puppet and I told stories to the children of Penasquitos Christian Preschool in San Diego during our chapel times which took place on a weekly basis during the school year. Three identical chapels held at different times enabled nearly 250 children (ages 3-5) to participate.

Chapel time would begin with the children and their teachers coming from their classrooms through the open doors of the church happily singing, "Jesus loves me this I know..." Jeremiah and I would join them and together we would sing three or four more spirited children's songs. Jeremiah would then assist me in telling an inspirational story to the children who were seated on colorful rugs up front.

Following the story children who were celebrating birthdays that week would be invited to join us and all of us would sing the Happy Birthday song. Then our friends would be reminded, "If you like you may have a birthday kiss from Jeremiah." Most would smile and nod, some would opt for a hug and still others would request both a hug and a kiss. We would conclude our worship time with prayer. Children had discussed their prayer concerns with their teacher before coming to chapel. The teachers would write them down on a piece of paper and the preschoolers would hand them to me. We always concluded with the same prayer: "Thank you Jesus for loving us. Now help us to love each other."

Initially we had five or six parents sitting in on the service. As time went on more and more parents and grandparents stayed around for chapel time. Eventually it was not unusual for forty or fifty adults to join us. It soon became obvious that although our chapel chats were intended for preschoolers, grown-ups were tuning in, too, so the message needed to be applicable to them as well.

What follows is a brief history of how Jeremiah became such an integral part of our ministry. I purchased this koala puppet at an auction fundraiser. I introduced myself and my koala to the children as they came to chapel for the first time in the new school year.

They were told a sad story of how he was obviously a very lonely and unhappy koala. However, we could make everything so much better if we could only find a family for him. Soon some children shouted out that he could join their family. The end result was that we all joyfully agreed that he would be welcomed into the preschool family.

Now it was very important that the family give him a good name. The children were instructed to discuss this with their teachers, make suggestions as to what his name should be, arrive at a consensus, then at our next chapel we could have a naming ceremony. We would make it very special and officially welcome him into the family. Several suggested that "Jeremiah" would be a good name for him. Soon everyone agreed.

Jeremiah's method of communicating is through facial gestures and whispering to me. He has even been on a mission trip to India where he brought joy and laughter to hundreds of Indian children (and adults, too).

Most of the stories in this book were told numerous times over a period of twenty years. Each school year brought new preschoolers and old stories were retold. Betsey Peck, preschool director, suggested that these stories be written down and shared with future classes. As I wrote these chapel chats in preparation for this book, I struggled to remember which stories originated with me and which were borrowed from other story tellers. I have attempted to give proper credit where I was aware of the source through notes taken years ago.

"I tell you the truth, anyone who will not receive the kingdom of God like a little child will never enter it." Mark 10:15

Visual Aid:
Scarf to cover
Jeremiah's face

WHEN YOU'RE AFRAID

Setting: Jeremiah is being introduced to the children for the first time. {enter the room with Jeremiah's face hidden covered with a scarf}

Hello, friends, I'm {name} and I'm excited to be here and ready to tell you a story. Is that something you would like? Good. My friend Jeremiah, the world's most loved koala puppet, will help me with the story. Jeremiah, are you ready? No? What's the matter? Why are you hiding your face? Please tell me. Oh, alright then, whisper it in my ear. {whisper} What? He told me that he's afraid. Jeremiah, there is no reason to be afraid. No one here will hurt you. These are very nice children and I think they would all like to be your friend. {whisper} You're not so sure that is true? You don't know any of these children and you are afraid that they won't like you? Jeremiah, I think that is a foolish fear. I'm quite sure that they will like you and you will soon have many new friends. Please don't be shy. You have no reason to be frightened. {Jeremiah doesn't move}

I haven't persuaded you yet, have I? You're still hiding your face. What do I need to do to prove to you that these children are eager to become your friends?

I have an idea. Here is what I plan to do. I'm going to remove the covering over your face and then I want you to lift your head

15

up and then slowly turn around and face the children. If you see even one person smiling you will know that your fears were unfounded and that you have met a friend. Are you ready? Here we go. I sure hope that we will see at least one smiling face, at least one person who wants to be your friend.

{remove scarf as Jeremiah cautiously turns to face the children} Look! Jeremiah, look! What do you see? There are smiles everywhere. Wow! One, two, three—so many more smiles I can't even count all of them. See! I told you they would like you and want to be your friend. It's wonderful. You had no reason to be afraid.

That's right, Jeremiah had no reason to be afraid. Often strangers are just friends that we haven't met yet.

Visual Aids:
Umbrella
Scissors
Cell Phone

ALL ARE NEEDED

Jeremiah, what am I holding? {umbrella} Of course, it is an umbrella. You never know when it might rain. I actually have two. I keep one in my car and another one at home. I've had this one for a long time. It has done a good job of keeping me dry.

Here I have scissors. {scissors} This is a very helpful tool as many of you know. I use it to cut paper or the stem of a fresh rose or even to trim my mustache. Every family benefits from having a good pair of scissors.

Do you know what this is? {cell phone} It is a cell phone. For many years I never had one. After I finally got one I discovered how useful it is. It helps me stay in touch with my family and friends. It goes with me just about everywhere I go. I seldom leave home without it.

All these items are special in their own way. The umbrella is always ready to help in rainy weather. The scissors take care of all my cutting and trimming needs. The cell phone enables me to stay connected to many special people. They don't have much in common but for each one there comes a time when they are needed. Each has a distinct and unique purpose. Could you imagine the problem my umbrella would have trying to cut some paper? Or my scissors attempting to keep me connected to my friends? Or my cell phone struggling to keep my head from getting wet during a rainy day? Each was made with a specific purpose in mind.

That's the way it is in Jesus' family. We are quite different but everyone is needed. When each of us is using our unique gifts then we complement each other and a lot of good is done.

As the Bible states, "the hand cannot say to the foot, I don't need you. Or the ear saying to the eye, I don't need you." No, all parts are needed and valued.

That is the way God made us. Some things you can do better than others and some things others can do better than you but both are needed and are important. Working together, using a wide variety of interests and gifts, so much good can be accomplished.

I know God smiles when He sees all of us helping in whatever way we can.

Visual Aids:
Photo of child crying

JESUS' TEARS

Jeremiah, do you see what I have today? {hold up picture} It is a sad picture, isn't it? I wonder why she is crying? It is possible, I suppose, that she has fallen down and skinned her knee. Ouch! That would bring tears. Maybe she is weeping because she is scared. A great big dog just barked at her and filled her with fears or it could be that she was going some place with other children and suddenly discovered that she was lost and alone. She could be crying for any number of reasons.

Is it true that little girls cry sometimes? Of course. Do little boys cry sometimes? Of course. They, too, could be in pain or afraid or disappointed. There are many reasons why a child might cry.

However, do adults ever cry? Do your mom and dad ever shed tears? Maybe you haven't seen it but I know they do. They may weep if their children are suffering or if a loved one dies.

But what about Jesus? Do you think He ever cried? This might surprise you but the answer is yes. A long time ago Jesus stood on a hill overlooking the great and holy city of Jerusalem. He observed masses of people coming and going into and out of the city and Jesus wept. It was not the kind of crying that happens when someone is in pain or afraid. No, Jesus was crying because He was so very sad. The people that He loved were so busy, so occupied with so many things that they had no time for God. God had been forgotten.

Jesus knew how much fear, hopelessness, and needless pain they would bear all because God had been forgotten.

We, too, can bring tears to the eyes of Jesus when we get so distracted by other things that we forget about Him.

But, and this is something I hope our friends will never forget, when we remember Jesus and place Him in the very center of our lives, peace and joy return and Jesus smiles.

Visual Aids:
Rose-colored glasses

GOD IS COLORBLIND

Jeremiah, look what happens when I take these glasses and hold it over your eyes. I look red and so does everything you see. When any of us look through these rose-colored glasses we see only one color: red.

Did you know that some animals cannot see certain colors and that millions of men (and some women, too) have eyes that cannot recognize red or green or other colors? We call such a condition colorblindness. Certain colors simply cannot be recognized.

However, Jeremiah, I have read that koalas like you see even better than most people do. You are quite fortunate.

Did you know that God is colorblind? Oh, not like people who can't see red or green. What I mean is that when God looks at us He doesn't see what color our skin is. He doesn't see black people or brown people or white people or yellow people. He only sees people! People that He loves very much.

It is His will that we should all be colorblind like that. We should see people through God's eyes. A great leader, Martin Luther King, Jr., proclaimed, "People should be judged not by the color of their skin but by the content of their character." He told us exactly what God wanted us to hear.

Did you know that most children are colorblind? That does not mean that they can't tell the difference between red and green. What it means is that they don't let a person's skin color stand in the way of friendship.

Sadly, though, there are grownups who sometimes do. Nevertheless, God has made it very, very clear. He wants all of us to be colorblind when it comes to the color of someone's skin. After all, He is the Father of all races and desires us to love each other as brothers and sisters who have the same Father.

WE'RE SPECIAL

Jeremiah, every one here brought with them what we're going to talk about today: our thumb.

Let's ask everyone to look at their hands. A hand is wonderful and fascinating, isn't it? It has four fingers and a thumb and each one moves by itself. You can tell your little finger to wiggle and it obeys. {wiggle finger} See. It will do exactly what you want it to do.

Now take a look at the index finger. We usually use it for pointing. {point} It is a finger we use a lot. We punch buttons on the phone, the elevator, and the computer. It is a valuable and busy finger because we use it so much.

But that which really separates us from nearly all other living things, besides our brain and our soul, is our thumb. Hardly any other creatures have thumbs, and the few that do are not nearly as skilled as we are in using our thumbs.

Have you ever tried to pick up something without using your thumb? It is possible {try it} but it certainly is awkward and difficult. I wouldn't want to even try to pick up a large drink without using my thumb.

Out thumb is called an "opposing digit." Now I know that is a strange term but it simply means that the thumb is opposite our fingers and comes to meet them. {demonstrate} Because that is true we are able to do good things with our hands that animals cannot do.

God has distinguished us from everything else He made by giving us incredible thumbs. Did you also know that your thumbs and mine are very distinct from each other? That's true. No two people have the same thumb prints. That is amazing when we remember that there are billions of people in this world.

Every now and then try picking up something without using your thumb. Then take a good look at your thumb and remember how unique you are. God made you unique and very special. He loves you just as you are and wants to be loved by you.

Visual Aids:

Stuffed Animal

Box of toys

GIVING THE BEST

Jeremiah, today we will tell a story about a precious young lady whose name was Emma. She had a favorite stuffed animal, like this one. {stuffed animal} She called him Sparky. Someone once frowned and exclaimed, "that's only a toy." But Emma knew better and treated Sparky as a good friend.

When Emma went to bed, guess who was on the pillow next to her? Yes, Sparky. When she went on a trip with her family, guess who sat beside her? You're right, Sparky. Whenever she watched TV, who do you suppose was on her lap? You're right again. It was Sparky. It seemed like no matter where she went or what she did, Sparky was always there.

Emma had another good friend, Sarah, who lived right next door. They played together nearly every day. They went to the same school and could usually be seen walking side-by-side. They loved each other and had so many happy times together.

One day, however, Emma received some very sad news. Sarah and her family would soon be moving to Texas. Her heart was breaking. Texas was so very far away. She didn't know when she'd ever see her friend again. Then she had an idea. She would give Sarah a going-away gift, something so special that Sarah would never forget their friendship. But what could that be?

She got out her toy box and started sifting through all her treasures. Surely she would find something there that would be a wonderful, never-to-be forgotten present for her friend. {box of variety of toys} She reached for a pair of red dancing shoes. They brought back lots of happy memories. She and Sarah were in the same dancing school- but, no, they were not special enough. How about a beautiful princess doll? Sarah had once commented how nice she thought the doll was. She knew it was something her friend would like but it just wasn't special enough.

Finally, after giving it deep, deep thought she decided what she would do to show her friend how much she loved her. She would give her the best she had. She would give her Sparky.

It was an incredible prize, an act of love, coming right from the heart. Sarah gasped with astonishment. She immediately recognized what a sacrificial gift this was and how much Emma loved her.

Well, Jeremiah, and boys and girls, when God wanted us to know how much we are loved he looked all around heaven for the very best gift for us. He gave us Jesus. The most wonderful gift he could possible give. "For God so loved the world-that's you and me-that he gave His only son..."

God help us to remember the precious gift of love he gave us when we received Jesus and may we joyfully share that love with others.

Visual Aid:

Several small sticks, strong stick, & a rod

HELP IN TIME OF TEMPTATION

Jeremiah, do you remember when we pray the Lord's Prayer we always pray "lead us not into temptation"? It is a daily prayer because temptation, that is when we're pulled or enticed to do something that displeases God, comes so often.

Let's pretend that this stick is you {hold up little stick} and here comes the devil who is also called the tempter. You think that you are strong enough to resist him. {wave stick} But the devil just smiles. He knows that he is much stronger than you are . {suddenly snap stick in half} The tempter breaks you easily.

Later you are a little older and a little stronger and think that you can win out over temptation. Here comes the tempter again. {wave stick in defiance} Once again the devil laughs at your futile effort to defeat him and quickly wins the battle. {snap stick in half}

What are you going to do? It seems that to resist temptation is a hopeless cause. A short time passes and suddenly the tempter appears confident that you'll be easily broken again. This time, however, you don't try to fight him alone but quickly go to Jesus and stand right next to him.

Now it is impossible for the devil to break you because Jesus is by your side. {make mighty but fruitless effort to break stick now next to big stick/rod}

Jesus is like the big stick. He is stronger than the devil. The devil cannot break Him and when we're with Jesus we cannot be broken.

When we ask Jesus to help us He usually sends other Christians to aid us and will use His power through them. We never have to fight these battles alone. Jesus has promised to fight our battles for us. Never again do we have to be afraid of the devil.

Visual Aids:

Bible

Sealed Envelope

A LETTER FOR ME?

Jeremiah, today's story is one that I read many years ago. It was written by Pastor Eldon Weisheit who is now telling his children's stories to angels up in heaven. I have made some changes in this story but he deserves the credit for much of it.

I'm sure that most of the mail that comes to your house is for your father or mother. But once in awhile there may be a letter for you. Here is one right now. {hold up sealed envelope} If this was for you what would you do with it? Would you decide to put it aside and maybe open it tomorrow? Would you wait to open it until sometime next week? Maybe you'd consider putting it in a picture frame on your desk? Of course not. That would be very foolish. Mail is to be read. Surely you would open your letter and read it. We read all the letters we receive, or do we?

The Bible is a letter from God to you, to me and to others. Way too many people leave the Bible unopened and unread. Others read the Bible as if they were reading someone else's mail. They don't apply it to their own lives. What about you? Do you know that the Bible is God's letter to you?

Yes. You can know that it is addressed to you even if it doesn't have your name and address on the cover. Instead of listing all the names of all the people for whom the Bible is intended, it describes the people. It is sent to sinners, to those that have failed to live up to God's plans for their lives. That is you and I. But it doesn't just tell us that we are sinners. It has good news. We read that Jesus loves and forgives sinners. It says that He gives them hope and a future.

Since it is God's letter to you, you should read it or listen to it as though God was speaking to you. The letter will say, "Finn, honor your father and mother." "Luke, don't bear false witness-don't ever lie." Remember to always read the Bible with you in mind. "By grace, Emma is saved through faith, it is the gift of God."

When you read the Bible that way you won't forget to keep on reading every day your mail from God.

A letter for me? Oh yes. The Bible is God's letter to you.

33

SECRET OF JOY

Jeremiah, did you miss me? I was gone for two weeks. Marcia and I went to visit our son Ben and his family in Florida and then to Virginia to spend some time with our son Rod and his family. We had great fun playing with our five grandchildren.

I understand that you and Mrs. Peck, our Penasquitos Christian Preschool director, shared a good story about the meaning of joy. Will you please retell it for me now?

This is the story that I heard. It was about a little boy, Jonathan, who was working hard to button his own shirt. Slowly and carefully he slid each button into a buttonhole. He finished and proudly looked at himself in a mirror. He was dismayed by what he saw. His shirt was all crooked. He thought he had put all the buttons in correctly in the right order. To be sure, he had done quite well except for one glaring mistake. The first button was in the wrong buttonhole. As a result, all of the other buttons were in wrong buttonholes. {hold up mis-buttoned shirt}

Jesus said, "Seek first God's will and God's plans and everything else will be taken care of for you." You see if God is not first, if His will is not our number one goal, then everything else that we do will be out of order no matter how diligently we strive to do it well.

Here is a helpful little guideline for us to follow to make certain everything is in its right order. Always spell the word JOY correctly. This is what I mean by that. Remember for true joy, the J must always come first. The J stands for Jesus. The next letter in joy is the O-others come next. Finally we have the Y-that's you. If we get the letters out of order joy is gone. If we keep the letters in the right order joy remains.

Jesus, others, you. That is the key to lasting joy.

Visual Aids:

Telephone

TELEPHONE CONVERSATIONS WITH GOD

Jeremiah, do you realize that just about everybody knows how to use a telephone? I'm amazed that even small children have learned how to make a phone call.

When you think about it you have to admit that it is a rather fascinating instrument. Simply by punching in a few numbers you are able to talk with your friend, Finn, in another city or your grandmother in a state far away or even your cousin Andrew in Australia.

I don't understand how I can pick up a telephone and talk with someone hundreds of miles away and they can talk to me. Oh, I know about telephone lines and I have read about specially designed fiber optics, but I still don't understand how it works. I just know it does.

Is it possible to even have a telephone conversation with God? Not exactly, but the Bible tells us that there is a way of talking with God that is much better that a phone call. It is called prayer. When we have a conversation with God we don't have to be in a certain place. As you may know there are some locations where there are no phones or where telephones won't work. But there is no place where you can't talk to God. You are able to pray anytime and anywhere.

There is something else that is worth remembering. When you talk to God the line is never busy. On occasion when we use the phone we hear a busy signal. That means that someone else is already using the phone so we will have to wait. But you never get a busy signal when you want to talk to God. He is always available, ready and eager to hear from you.

Have you ever punched in a wrong number? I have. If your fingers make just one mistake you get the wrong person. That never happens when you pray. You always get the right person.

I don't understand prayer. I don't know how I can talk to God but I know I can and I know He hears me.

It is also very important for all of us to remember that every telephone has two parts. There is a place to speak and a place to listen. So how do we listen to God? There are several different ways. Sometimes through our conscience we hear in our hearts a still, small voice giving us guidance. At other times it will come through a deep feeling of inner peace that comes after prayer in which we sense that everything is going to be alright. Many times God will choose to speak to us through our parents or other godly people. Of course He most frequently speaks to us through His written word, the Bible.

It is a very good idea to conclude our conversation with God, our prayer, by adding these words, "I'm so glad I could spend this time talking with You. Is there anything you want to say to me now? I'm listening." It is amazing what we might hear.

Visual Aids:
3 Photos of your children,
wedding, parents

TRINITY

Jeremiah, recently I was visiting with young man, Andrew, talking about God, when he asked me if I could help him understand what we mean when we say we believe in the Trinity. It was a good question and not an easy one to answer since the Trinity will always be somewhat of a mystery. I attempted to answer his question with a personal example.

Who am I? I am a combination of many things. For example, I am a father. I have two sons, Rod and Ben. {hold photo} That is an important part of my identity. I am a father.

I am also a husband. I became a husband on the day I married Marcia. {wedding photo} As the Bible declares, "For the two shall become one." I cannot separate myself from my oneness with my wife. She is an integral part of who I am.

I am also a son. {hold photo with parents} My parents would testify that I am their son and if medical proof were needed a DNA sample would verify it. I will always be a son.

I am only one person but I am also 100% father, 100% husband, 100% son, like three persons in one. God is Father, Son, and Holy Spirit, three persons in one, distinctly revealed in three different ways. All Christians believe in the Trinity.

The Father is the Creator who made heaven and earth. He made us and still takes care of us and provides us with all that we need. For all of this and so much more it is our duty to thank, praise, serve and obey Him.

The Son is Jesus, our Lord, who was born of the Virgin Mary, and paid the penalty for our sins by dying on the cross. He rose from the dead. He will come again as King of Kings and Lord of Lords to judge the world. Surely as a result of such amazing love and grace we will want to be His faithful followers.

The Holy Spirit is our Counsellor, our guide, and the power of God who purifies us, forgives us and calls us through His Word, the Bible, to be His disciples.

So, there it is, Jeremiah, an illustration about the Trinity which I hope will give us a glance into this holy mystery. The Trinity is a term we use to help explain how God has shown Himself to us in three different ways.

Visual Aids:

4 hats (firefighter, hardhat,

military, baker/chef)

HOW TO TELL WHAT A PERSON DOES

Jeremiah, oftentimes we can tell what a person does by the hat he is wearing. For example, if you saw someone with a hat like this {firefighter's helmet} what do you think he does? Right! A firefighter.

How about this hat? What kind of work does someone do while wearing a hat like this? {chef} You are right again. A chef or baker wears a hat just like this one.

In our community quite a few people go to work wearing caps like this, including my son, Rod. {military} Of course it is the cap worn in the Navy.

Suppose your neighbor climbs into his pickup truck and heads for work with this on his head. {hard hat} Jeremiah, they guessed correctly again. He is a construction worker or a builder.

We can often tell what people do by the hats they wear. What about your teacher? How would anyone know what she does since she doesn't wear a hat? You would have to watch her and listen to her before you would discover that she is a teacher. In like manner we Christians don't have special hats that we wear declaring that we are followers of Jesus. So then how will people know who we are? I would hope that others could look at us and say, "Do you see how they share and do you hear what they say

41

and have you watched how they live and something else; have you noticed how loving they are? They must be followers of Jesus."

We don't need to wear a special identification cap to tell people that we are Christians. Our words and our actions should clearly announce who we are.

WHY IS THE DEAD SEA DEAD?

Jeremiah, a few days ago a boy named Finn asked me if I'd ever heard of the Dead Sea. When I said yes, he wanted to know what made it sick and how it died. That was a very interesting question. The Dead Sea is located in the Holy Land on the other side of the world and it is the lowest spot on earth. In the water there is a lot of salt, just as there is in the ocean, but the water in the Dead Sea has no place to go and just gets saltier and saltier until nothing can live in it. There is not one plant or one fish in it and if we put one there it would soon die.

There is an important lesson that can be learned from this. It is explained to us in a popular parable that first appeared in the ancient Midrash Rabbah many centuries ago.

The parable starts by reminding us that there are two seas in Israel. One is fresh and fish live in it. Splashes of green adorn its banks. Along its shores the children play.

The river Jordan makes this sea with sparkling water from the hills, so it laughs in the sunshine and people build their houses near it, and the birds their nests; and every kind of life is happier because it is there.

The river Jordan flows south into another sea. Here there is no splash of fish, no dancing leaf, no song of birds, and no children's laughter. Travelers choose another route unless on urgent business. No person, animal, or bird will drink from its waters.

What makes the difference? Not the river Jordan. It empties the same good water into both. Not the soil in which they lie, and not the surrounding country. No, the difference is that one receives the refreshing water of the Jordan but does not keep it. For every drop that flows in another drop flows out. The other sea hoards everything it receives. Every drop it receives it keeps. The Sea of Galilee gives and lives. The other sea gives nothing. It is called the Dead Sea.

Jeremiah, there are two kinds of people just as there are two kinds of seas in Israel. There are those who receive blessings from God and pass them on to others. And there are those who try to keep them all for themselves. Eventually their spirit dries up and dies.

The good Sea of Galilee has set a wonderful example for us. It continues to thrive and be a blessing because it shares. When we share our blessings our life sparkles and the blessings keep coming to us and going on through us to others.

Visual Aids:

1st class postage stamp, envelope

MARKED FOR SERVICE

Jeremiah, many years ago I remember reading a small book titled " One Minute with God." The author, Bill Lampkin, had written many inspiring devotional thoughts. One tale in particular stood out in my mind so I took some notes thinking that someday I would retell it. It was a very brief story about a postage stamp. I hope I can tell it as well as the author did so long ago.

A dad named Ben gave his son, Luke, a dollar and a letter and sent him to the Post Office to buy a stamp and mail the letter. Soon Luke came back with a very proud look on his face. Handing his father the dollar he said, "I saved us some money. Nobody was looking so I mailed the letter without the stamp."

Did the boy's plan work? Of course not. That letter came back to his father's house since the street number was on the return address label and he had to put a stamp on it and mail it all over again. Of course that made it several days late. I imagine that Luke and his father had quite a conversation as his father explained to him how the postal service works.

Here is a first class postage stamp that is in its proper place on the envelope which is addressed and ready to go. {do it} It declares to everyone that someone cares for the contents of the letter.

Please note: it is marked for service and has a destination. Can you think of a mark that followers of Jesus have that says they are ready to serve? The answer is baptism. Every Christian is baptized and marked with the sign of the cross. We have been marked to serve.

What is our destination? When life concludes where do we want to go? We want to go to heaven where we will be in the presence of Jesus forever. We're on our way and marked for service. We don't know exactly where the road will take us or how long the journey may be. We are called "Followers of the Way" because Jesus said, "I am the Way" and we are following Jesus wherever He may lead us.

Next time you see a stamp on a letter ready to be mailed, think of the stamp you bear and where you are going and all the service you can do for God along the way.

OUR TONGUE

Jeremiah, you and I had a wonderful time on our mission trip to India, didn't we? It soon became obvious that the Indian children loved you almost as much as you are loved by all our friends here. You were a great traveler and put a smile on so many faces. As a matter of fact, I'm sure Jesus was smiling, too.

While we were gone Pastor Greg led our chapel service. He told the following story: today I'm going to talk about something everyone of us has. You brought it with you this morning and so did I. It is claimed to be the strongest muscle that we have.

What do you think I'm talking about? Is it your arm? {flex muscle} No, some have very strong arm muscles but it is not the strongest muscle in your body. Maybe it is your leg muscle. {kick your leg} No, that was another good guess but it is not correct.

Many believe that the strongest muscle in your body is your tongue. {point to your tongue} That is a surprise, isn't it? One of the reasons the tongue is the strongest muscle is because it gets so much exercise.

How do we exercise out tongue? We use it to taste. Put a piece of chocolate in your mouth and the flavor tastes sweet, doesn't it? What about some lemon juice? Right away we know it is sour. Our tongue is for tasting.

Our tongue always helps us to swallow. While we are eating our tongue helps to move the food around in our mouth and send it down into our stomach.

Even though our tongue is very small it controls the whole body. That is because every word we speak tells something about who we are. Our tongue leads us when we pray our prayers, say kind words, sing praises, and express thanks. With our tongue we can say, "God bless you" and "I love you."

Our tongue is a wonderful gift from God when we use it as He intended. It is one of the most vital and important parts of our body.

Jesus healed a man who couldn't hear or speak and then He told him to "go and tell your friends the wonderful things God has done for you."

That is a marvelous way to use the strongest muscle in our body. Our tongue is a powerful muscle for good when it is used to tell our friends of Jesus and His love.

The final reminder: Your tongue can be God's tongue in your mouth singing His praises and sharing good news.

INVITATION TO A WEDDING

Jeremiah, I received an invitation this week to a wedding. {read it out loud} I will be there to rejoice with a young couple as they exchange their wedding vows. It promises to be a time of joy and I am honored to be included.

Thinking about this wedding reminded me of a wedding that we read about in the Bible. A wedding that was attended by Jesus and some of his disciples.

John writes that there was going to be a wedding in Cana and Jesus was invited. That informs us of something very positive about this bride and groom, doesn't it? They were going to become husband and wife and they wanted Jesus to share in their joy. He gladly accepted their offer, He always does, and was there to bless them with His presence.

Word was received that the wedding party had run out of wine. The refreshments were all gone. It was an embarrassing and unhappy time for the hosts. But that is when Jesus chose to perform His first miracle. He turned water into wine. Now, thanks to Jesus, they had plenty of delicious refreshments.

Once after a child heard this story he was asked what he learned from it. This was his reply, "I learned that if you are going to be married be sure that you invite Jesus to the wedding." He had learned a powerful lesson. Certainly good advice for all of us.

There is something else about this wedding that is often overlooked but it is important. When this bridal couple sent out their wedding invitations they not only invited Jesus but they invited some of his friends, too.

I think this is critical because some people seem to think they can have Jesus all to themselves. They're not interested in His friends. This is a big, big mistake. Jesus himself said you can't really love God if you don't love his people.

The lesson here is that when we invite Jesus to be our friend, we also invite all His followers to be our friends.

When Jesus sees Christians-that's us-loving and caring for each other, He smiles and is happy. One of the ways that we show our love for Him is by loving one another

MEANING OF LIFE

One day while Jeremiah and I were traveling together we came across this object. {frisbee} We looked at each other and asked, "What is this?" It was not very heavy, round, brightly colored and made of plastic. What was its purpose? You probably know what this is but Jeremiah and I could only guess.

We gazed at the object for awhile and then Jeremiah suggested that it might be a hat. {put it on Jeremiah's head} Jeremiah, as soon as you moved your head it fell off. I don't know what it is but it certainly doesn't make a very good hat.

Do you have any more ideas? You think it might be a nice decoration to put on our front door? Well it does look a bit like a rising sun but surely it has a higher purpose that just a decoration to look at now and then.

You know what I think, Jeremiah? It might be possible that this is a little sled. That's right, you sit on it and slide down a snow bank. {sit on it—fall off} Whoa! That didn't work at all. It was never intended to be a sled so what is it?

Just then our friend Andrew came by and said with a big smile, "Wow! You have found a neat frisbee. Toss it to me."

Then it dawned on us what the manufacturer had in mind when it was made. It was designed to be a toy for us to play with. We could sail it to each other, high and low, up and down and have lots of fun. Even Bosun, our chocolate lab, enjoyed chasing and catching the frisbee. Once we understood why the frisbee had been made we had a wonderful time with it.

Well, Jeremiah, there are many people in this world who don't know why they are here. They have no idea why God created them. They will try to do something then switch to something else but are never satisfied. Day after day they struggle looking for meaning and purpose but never succeed in finding it. They grow older sensing that something is missing. There is an aimlessness and absence of joy. Their whole life is a fruitless effort to discover who they are and why they are here.

But, Jeremiah. we know why we are here, don't we? God has made it very clear. We are here to love God and love each other. That's it. That is the number one reason God made us. How we demonstrate that love will not always be the same since He has given us unique personalities, interests, and abilities. But His plan for all of us is the same. We are here to love God and to love each other.

Visual Aids:
Doctor's prescription, bottle of medicine

KNOWING AND DOING

Jeremiah, today I have a question for you and for our friends. However, before I ask the question let me tell you a story from the Bible.

A long time ago people used to ask Jesus very hard questions to see if He really knew what He was talking about. For example, one day He was asked if it were possible to live forever. He answered by saying, "Look in your Bible. What does it say?" The man who asked the question responded, "Yes, that's what the Bible says." Jesus replied, "You know the Bible is true so now do what it says."

It doesn't make much difference if we know what we should do if we don't do it. For instance, let's suppose that I had a bad stomach-ache and so my doctor gave me a prescription for some medicine that would make me feel better. I then took the prescription to the drug store to get my medicine. I paid for it, went home, followed the directions on the bottle, took the proper dosage and was soon on the road to recovery.

Now, this is the question I have for you. When did I start getting well? When I went to the doctor? After I got the prescription? When I left to go to the drugstore or when I actually took the medicine? To get well I needed to do all these things, didn't I? Yet nothing I did would have been of any value had I not truly taken the medicine.

That is what Jesus told the man who asked the question about everlasting life. You start by knowing what the Bible says but until you really do what it says it doesn't do you any good.

"Proof that you love me," Jesus said, "is that you do what I asked you to do."

What is the first and most important thing that Jesus asked us to do? Anybody know? Jeremiah, do you think that you could tell us what it is? {Jeremiah whispers in my ear}

Jeremiah said our Lord wants us to love God and to love each other. Jeremiah is absolutely right! When Jesus sees such love then He knows that we are His faithful followers and His heart is filled with joy.

Visual aid:

Child

WHO IS THE GREATEST?

Jeremiah, in our story today we are going to discuss who is the greatest. Years ago a champion boxer after winning a fight would raise his arms {flex muscles} and shout, "I am the greatest!"

He wasn't the only one to brag about himself like that. Throughout history there have been many boasting that they were the greatest.

Jeremiah, who do you think is the greatest? Is it a person who is big and powerful like a giant? Maybe it is someone who has millions and millions of dollars? A singer who is so popular that crowds will stand in line for hours to buy a ticket to her concert? Who is the greatest? I wonder how Jesus would answer that question.

In the Gospel of Matthew we read that the disciples were having an argument about which one of them would be the greatest in the kingdom of heaven. Jesus overheard their heated conversation and very disappointed, shook his head from side to side. "Listen to me," Jesus said, "and I will tell you what it means to be great."

Then he brought a child {select a small child} and put his arm around little Jonathan and declared, "Unless you change and become like this little child you will not enter the kingdom of heaven. Whoever humbles himself like this child is the greatest in the kingdom of heaven."

On one other occasion Jesus had stressed the importance of children. It happened this way: parents were bringing their children to Jesus so He could bless them and hug them. Some of the disciples were upset by this interruption and told the parents to take their children home. After all, Jesus was too important to waste his precious time with children. When Jesus heard what they were doing He was very angry, "Stop that! I love children. Bring them to me." Then He told the disciples and all the people that if they would be great in the eyes of God they must be like little children.

The traits of little children that Jesus so admired surely include the following: the unrestricted enthusiasm of healthy children who don't just walk. They run, hop, skip, jump and dance with joy for life. They soon recognize they were not made to do it alone but need the help of others; how quickly they make friends, ignoring skin color, dress, accent or anything else which is often a barrier for grownups. The prayers of these little ones are filled with words of thanks. Perhaps above all they are humble and trusting.

In the eyes of Jesus they and adults with these childlike traits are the greatest in the kingdom of heaven.

Visual Aids:

Cup with pencils in a variety of colors

A BEGGAR MEETS JESUS

Jeremiah, when I was a little boy I always enjoyed going just about anywhere with my dad. I loved to be with him-it made no difference where we were going-to the market, gas station, post office or especially the bank. I still have vivid memories of our visit to the bank.

Outside the bank's front door, sitting on a blanket, was a blind man. In front of him was a cup filled with brand new pencils in a variety of colors. He was hoping that bank customers would buy a pencil or two so that he would have a little money and be able to take care of himself. Since he could not see he could not get a job anywhere.

My dad would hand me a quarter and tell me to select a pencil. I would carefully choose a pencil that I thought we could use and then drop a quarter in his cup and tell him which pencil I had selected. He would always say, "Thank you, young man."

My dad said that by buying a pencil we helped this man have dignity. He wouldn't feel like a beggar. After all he offered something of value in exchange for our coins.

The Bible tells us a story about Bartimeus, a blind beggar.

{have children tightly close their eyes} For Bartimeus every day was like a day with your eyes closed. Nothing could be seen. How very sad.

This poor man would often sit by the roadside holding out a cup, pleading with those who were passing by to drop in a coin or two so he would have a little money and be able to buy something to eat.

Bartimeus had heard many amazing stories about Jesus including the exciting news that Jesus had healed sick people and even given sight to the blind. He desperately hoped that someday he would meet Jesus. That day finally came. He listened to the sounds of a large crowd approaching and he heard them mention the name Jesus.

The noise grew louder as the crowd got closer. In desperation he loudly cried out, "Jesus, help me! Have mercy on me!" Those standing near him told him to be quiet. But he just yelled all the louder.

Jesus heard him, saw him, and then came over to him and asked him what he wanted. How do you think the blind beggar answered that question? You're right. He told Jesus that he wanted his eyes to be opened so that he could see. Jesus answered his prayer. He received his sight. He was no longer blind. He could see!

From that day on a happy and thankful former beggar and blind man became a follower of Jesus. The Bible declares that Bartimeus told everyone he met what Jesus had done for him.

It is a truly wonderful story. It reminds us that God has blessed us with eyes that see and we want to always be thankful for that. Like Bartimeus, the former beggar, we can joyfully let others know what Jesus has done for us.

PICKING UP PENNIES

Jeremiah, a man by the name of James Tedder, told the following story about picking up lost pennies. I think it is a very good story and I hope our friends will like it, too.

He said that once a friend of his and his friend's wife were invited to spend the day with his employer who was a very wealthy man. He was also a very generous man and took this young couple to a wonderful Broadway show where they had excellent seats, right up front. It was something they never would have been able to do on their own because it was way too expensive.

After the play was over they got into his brand new Lexus and headed for a very exclusive dining experience. The valet parked their car and they started walking toward the restaurant when, quite suddenly, the boss stopped and looked intently at an object on the pavement near the curb.

The employer saw something that the others couldn't see or so they thought. After all, there was nothing there except some paper litter and an old penny. Silently he reached down and picked up the penny. He held it up, smiled and then put it in his pocket as if he'd found a great treasure. How strange. Why would this rich man take the time to stop and pick up a penny?

Throughout the entire dinner that scene bugged the young lady. Finally she could stand it no longer so she asked him if he found a coin of some value. A smile was on his face as he reached into his pocket for the penny and held it out for her to see. She had seen many pennies before. What was the point of this?

"Look at it," he said, "Read what it says." She read the words, "United States of America." "No, not that, please keep reading." "One cent." "No, not that either. Keep reading." "In God we trust." "YES! You see if I trust in God the name of God is holy even on a coin. Whenever I find a coin I see the inscription. It is written on every U.S. coin. God drops a message right in front of me reminding me to trust Him. Who am I to pass it by? I pick up the coin as a response to God; yes, I do trust Him. I think it is God's way of starting a conversation with me. I am so thankful that God is patient and pennies are plentiful."

Jeremiah, isn't that a great idea? Sometimes we just need to slow down, stop our busy lives and feel God's presence. Sometimes we may need a little reminder, like a penny lying on the ground.

May each of us pick up a penny soon.

Visual Aids:

Grapes & raisins

BAD TO GOOD

Jeremiah, just about everyone likes sweet grapes, right? Well, maybe not koalas but most children enjoy eating grapes.

For a long time, before people had refrigeration, it was difficult to keep picked grapes fresh so most grapes grown in the old days were either immediately eaten or made into wine.

Some years ago there was a terrible drought in central California where there were many vineyards. One poor farmer looked at his skinny, seedless, shriveled-up grapes, obviously now useless for wine making, and apparently no good for anything else.

Nevertheless, not wanting to just throw them away, he sent them to a grocer in San Francisco and told him to sell them for any price. Now what could a grocer do with a box of bad grapes?

That must be a question God sometimes has to consider as He sees men and women, boys and girls do some bad and foolish things. Can any good come from such ugly behavior?

Let me tell you what the grocer did with those bad grapes. He left them out in the sun for a couple of days until they were completely dried out. Lo and behold, much to his surprise, he discovered that he had a box of very good tasting raisins. {hold up grapes, then pull out a box of raisins} Wow! What seemed like a disaster turned into a wonderful discovery.

That is how the raisin farming business in California was born. As a matter of fact this fortunate farmer's raisins became so popular that he called them his "Peruvian Delicacy" and soon was able to sell this tasty fruit for a high price.

That is the way God works, too. In the Bible, we read, "We know that in everything God works for good with those who love him..." God promises to bring good out of that which appears to be bad when it happens. But remember, his promise is for those who love him.

Visual Aids:
Chocolate bar &
box of candy

CHILDREN OBEY YOUR PARENTS

Jeremiah, usually Finn and Luke, ages 5 & 7, would walk to school together. It was about a ten minute walk to Rolling Hills School. The day came, however, when Finn was on a field trip so Luke was walking by himself.

He noticed a dark colored car, like an SUV, driving slowly toward him. He didn't think anything about it until the van stopped. Someone he didn't know, a stranger, rolled down the window and called out to him, "Hi, Sonny. I've got something here that I know you will like. See. It's a big chocolate bar. That's not all. For such a nice little guy like you I've got a whole bag of goodies." {goodies bag} He opened the door and with a smile on his face he said, "Hop in. I'll give you all this {candy} and a ride home."

All that stuff sure looked tasty. But then Luke remembered his parents told him to never accept gifts from strangers no matter what the gift might be. They also told him never, never, never get into a stranger's car. Why? Because sometimes a stranger has lied. Instead of being kind he has taken the child far from home where he hurt him or maybe refused to bring him home until the parents paid him lots of money.

Luke remembered what his parents had told him and even though the candy and other goodies looked appealing, he shouted, "No!" and started running away.

We are so thankful Luke obeyed his parents and refused to get into the stranger's car. If he had disobeyed his parents it could have been a tragic day for him and heart-breaking for his family.

The Bible says, "Children obey your parents." Parents give their children boundaries, that is, certain rules to follow and obey. I'm sure you've all been given some rules that you are expected to obey. Am I right? Of course I am. It is because your parents love you and want to protect and help you that their rules are so important.

Because Luke obeyed his parents he avoided possible evil and the story has a happy ending.

Visual Aids:
Some form of ID:
Driver's license or passport

WHO ARE YOU?

Jeremiah, it's been almost two thousand years since the greatest event in all of human history took place. Jesus Christ was resurrected from the dead. It is an amazing story, but more than that, it is the greatest story ever told and we never grow tired of hearing it again. The message of Easter. The grave has no victory. The sting has been removed from death.

John, one of the twelve apostles, writes that a week after Easter the disciples were gathered together rejoicing and celebrating the resurrection victory. All were excited and happy. Well, actually not all. There was one exception: Thomas. He was a disciple of Jesus, a great friend and a good man. However, he found it just too hard to believe that Jesus was alive. He had seen him put to death on a cross and buried in a tomb. His friends told him that Jesus was alive and that they had seen Him. It seemed to be too good to be true. He said that he had to have proof.

Sometimes people demand proof today that you are who you say you are. If I asked you to show me some identification what would you do? Identification is evidence that you are who you claim to be. When you are an adult and asked to show your ID you might display one of these: {show ID}, a driver's license or a passport or even a Social Security card. There are other forms of

ID too, but these are the main documents people will accept as proof of who you are.

Thomas wanted proof that Jesus was truly alive. He said that the only way he would believe that Jesus had actually conquered death was to see Jesus with his own eyes and he added, "put my fingers in the nail wounds and place my hand in the spear wound in his side."

Shortly after he had said that Jesus appeared: "Look at me, Thomas," Jesus said, "place your fingers in my wounds. I want you to believe. Here is your proof."

Thomas dropped to his knees and cried out, "My Lord and my God!" He had received all the proof he would ever need.

Jesus was happy that Thomas finally believed. Then he said, "Blessed are those who have not seen and yet believe." That's us. We believe what the Bible says and we know that our crucified Savior is alive and lives and reigns through all eternity. We are the most blessed of all.

NEVER ALONE

Jeremiah, I don't remember who it was who told a wonderful story in which she compared the work of a baby sitter to the work of the Holy Spirit. This morning I'm going to tell my version of that story and I'm going to ask Emma {teen-ager} to sit with us as we talk about the promise Jesus made before ascending into heaven.

Thank you, Emma, for helping us this morning. I have asked you here because of a job you do. I wonder if anyone can guess what it is? Maybe it is because she walks her dog every evening? Or because she helps to vacuum the carpets at home? Could it be because she helps wash the dishes? She works hard at many different tasks but I invited her up here because she is an excellent babysitter. We all know how important that is.

Whenever your parents go out and you have to stay at home someone needs to be there to take care of the children. Can you imagine what it would be like if no one was there with you? Oh, at first it might be fun since you could do anything that you wanted to do. But after awhile, it would get lonely and maybe even scary.

The most important responsibility of a babysitter or childcare provider, as they are sometimes called, is to take the place of your parents for a little while. They need to watch over you and take good care of you.

Just as your parents are concerned about you when they leave, Jesus was concerned about his disciples when He was ready to depart this world. He promised them that He would not leave them alone. Instead He would always be with them in a wonderful way through His Spirit. To a certain degree the Holy Spirit was like a divine babysitter who would be with them constantly and provide for all their needs.

That same promise is ours today. Jesus is with us through His Spirit. He speaks to us, comforts us, guides us, listens to us and loves us.

It is true that Jesus returned to heaven after the Easter resurrection victory and we often wish that we could see him with our eyes and touch him with our hands. But He is still very much with us just like a babysitter when parents are away.

He will never leave us alone. His Spirit will stay close always until the day that Jesus returns and takes us to heaven.

CAN'T MEASURE GOD'S LOVE

Jeremiah, my friend, today I have a measuring stick that is one yard long. With my measuring stick I can measure just about anything. Let's start with something easy. Let's measure my little finger. It's not very long, only three inches. Now we'll measure my foot. It's exactly one foot long. That's kind of funny, isn't it?

How about this chair? I would guess that it is about a foot and a half from the floor. That was a good guess because it is exactly right. Let's measure a person. Finn, we'd like to measure you, is that OK? Thank you. He is almost as long as our yardstick and of course he is still growing.

We can measure so many things. Do you think we could even measure a baseball diamond? Could we measure how far it is all around the bases to home plate? It is actually 360 feet so we would need 120 measuring sticks this size.

Jeremiah, we have instruments that can measure far more than our yardstick is able to do. As a matter of fact we have ways to measure tall buildings and high mountains. We are able to measure how far it is to the moon. It seems like we can measure anything, can't we?

Well, actually, no. We can't measure everything. How would it be possible to measure God's love? It is higher, deeper, wider than anything we could ever measure.

Jeremiah, oh how comforting it is to know how much God loves us. He loves us with an immeasurable love. He loves us with a love that never ends. He wants us to love each other with that same kind of unending love.

You know what, Jeremiah? We are able to love because we have been loved. Now, friends, stretch out your hands as wide as you possibly can. {stretch out hands} Now say to each other, "I love you this much."

God loves you and we all love each other and that means that Jeremiah and I love you very much, don't we, Jeremiah? I knew you would say YES!

Visual Aid:

Telephone

PRAYER IS CONVERSATION WITH GOD

Jeremiah, a family counseling center in our town likes to advertise that "help is as near as your phone." That sounds like good news. After all, my phone is right here. {hold up phone} So I certainly won't have to go very far when I need help, will I?

I guess that is partly true. If I need counseling or some advice I'm glad that I can just pick up my phone and speak to someone. But what if the help I need is an emergency because I injured myself? I can use the phone to call the paramedics but the phone itself is very restricted in how it can help me. It can't bandage wounds or hand out medicine.

Suppose there was a fire in my kitchen. I could use the phone to call the fire department but the phone itself could not put the fire out. Certainly it would be helpful but it couldn't provide all the help I needed.

I could also make a phone call to the police if there was a crisis, or to a plumber if a water pipe was broken and of course to the pest control person if I discovered termites in my garage. In each case the phone would be helpful but it really wouldn't erase my problems.

In some ways prayer is like a telephone only so much better. When you need help you can use the telephone to call someone. With prayer you can ask God for help and when you speak to Him you won't have to wait long for Him to respond. He won't ask for your address or be worried about a traffic jam while in route. Why? Because He is already with you, never having left, He will answer in an instant. He has said, "Don't be afraid. I'll never leave you."

Well, Jeremiah, you and I are both glad that we have access to a telephone, aren't we? It can be especially comforting during those times when we are alone. However, the phone's capacity to provide lasting help for us is very limited. Not so with prayer. There is nothing that is impossible for God. He has urged us to be in constant prayer and has promised to hear our prayers and to answer them. What greater help could anyone ever want?

Visual Aids:
2 glasses; 2 water-filled
bottles; red button;
red food coloring

A FAITH THAT CHANGES ALL OF LIFE

Jeremiah, I don't remember the lady's name but I do remember the story she told during Vacation Bible School. She explained the difference between two kinds of faith. One is a faith of great value, alive and strong. The other is a faith that is of little value.

So here I go repeating her story. The bottle represents you. Now I will add something to the water. {drop in a red button} The red represents faith now in your life. But sadly it is barely visible way down in the corner. Even though the red button is in the water it has not changed the water at all. {pour into glass} See, it remains the same as it was before I dropped the red button in it. In real life, if faith has not transformed how you live, if it can't be seen, then of what value is it? You can say that you have faith, like a bottle has a red button, but unless the faith touches every part of your life it is useless.

Let's look at another illustration. The second bottle is also your life. We again add red. {pour in red food coloring and shake bottle} This time the red changes all parts of the water. A living faith is the same in our lives. A strong, vigorous faith makes a big difference in every part of our lives. It becomes the heart of what we say, what we do, how we treat others and how we spend our money and our time. It has a powerful influence in all of life and in all of our decisions.

The water most recently poured into the glass has been permanently changed because the red stays in it. Faith in Jesus, a living faith, makes every day a day of blessing and gives hope, meaning and purpose to life. Such a faith also gives us courage and strength to be a blessing to others.

So, Jeremiah, each of us, no matter what our age, needs to examine our lives and ask the serious question, "Does my faith resemble the first bottle or the second bottle?"

Once when one of the disciples was examining his faith he saw how weak it was but he honestly wanted it to be stronger and so he prayed, "Jesus, increase my faith."

That would be a good prayer for all of us to pray.

SPIRITUAL LIFE JACKET

Jeremiah, it is another nice day and we have a story with a warning. I hope that you and all your friends will listen carefully.

Last summer Jonathan went on a vacation trip with his brother, Andrew, his sister, Emma, and his parents, of course. They were planning to spend a week at a lodge on Big Bear Lake. There they would be meeting his cousins, Luke and Finn. He could hardly wait to get there. He knew they were going to have so much fun.

Here is what happened soon after their arrival. The four older children ran down to the lake and with shouts of joy jumped in. Jonathan wanted to join them but he had not yet learned how to swim. It was a sad time for poor Jonathan. He just stood and watched the others frolicking in the water. Oh, how he wanted to join them but what could he do?

His parents had a answer to his problem. They put a life jacket on him. {hold up life jacket} They strapped it on securely. Now he was ready. His life jacket enabled him to float on top of the water. It was safe and easy and now he excitedly joined the others.

For several days he followed the same routine. After breakfast his life jacket was put on and into the cool water he would go with the other children.

One morning, however, he had trouble finding his life jacket. "Oh, well," he said to himself, "I don't have time to look for it.

I'll miss too much fun. Besides I don't think I need it anymore." So off to the lake he went and jumped right in. Immediately he started to sink. Down, down, down he went until his head disappeared under the water. He would have drowned if his big brother Andrew had not seen what happened and jumped in and rescued him.

It was very scary and a tough way to learn a lesson but it was a lesson he never forgot. Always wear a life jacket before going into deep water.

Well, Jeremiah, in somewhat the same way God has sent His son to be our life jacket. Each morning we need to start the day with a prayer that Jesus will support us, guide us and lead us.

Little Jonathan will soon learn to swim and will not need a life jacket but we cannot live our lives and have meaning and purpose without the presence of Jesus. No matter where we are or how old we are we will always need Jesus to hold us up.

Visual Aid:

Broken branch

LOVED EVEN WHEN WE DISOBEY

Jeremiah, today we're going to talk about a boy named Luke who disobeyed his father but, nevertheless, learned a powerful lesson.

One Sunday morning Luke's mother woke him up early and told him that she wanted him to put on his brand new pants and shirt so he'd look really nice for the first day of Sunday School.

He did as he as told and did look quite handsome. After church the whole family would be going out to have dinner with his grandparents at their home which was way out in the countryside. Luke always enjoyed those visits. His grandma made the best apple pie that he had ever tasted. Plus they lived on several acres of land so there were lots of neat places to play. Grandpa and Grandma also had a wonderful big happy dog named Maverick. Maverick loved to play fetch with a frisbee so Luke knew they were going to have lots of fun.

A delicious dinner was completed and Luke headed outside to play. His father reminded him, "Luke, you're wearing your brand new clothes today so please don't climb any trees. I wouldn't want your new outfit to get messed up." "OK, Daddy," he replied, "I'll stay out of the trees."

He played fetch with Maverick for a long time. They both enjoyed that but eventually Luke got tired and started looking around for something else to do.

He turned around and looked at those very old trees with low hanging branches. They were perfect for climbing. He had climbed them before and it had been great fun.

"But," he said to himself, "Daddy gave strict orders. There was to be no climbing today because I might mess up my new clothes."

Luke stood quietly by himself wondering what to do next. Those trees were so tempting. It was almost as if they were calling to him. He thought, "I know Daddy doesn't want me to climb any trees. He's afraid I'll mess up my new clothes but surely it wouldn't hurt anything if I was really very careful and just climbed up on one branch." So that is what he did. He smiled. No harm done. Beside no one would ever know that he was up on the tree. So he went up, higher and higher and higher until he was near the very top of the tree. He could see for a long way. This was so exciting!

Time to get down before anyone sees him. He carefully started making his way down when it happened! {break branch} He stepped on a branch and it broke off and its sharp edge tore a hole in his pants, trapping him way up in the tree. Now he was really scared, stuck to a broken branch with no way to get down.

Just then he heard his father calling, "Luke, where are you? It's time to go home." Oh, what a sickening feeling. Trapped way up in a tree where he wasn't supposed to be, frightened and ashamed, yet he knew that without Daddy's help he could never get down safely.

In a shaking voice he called down, "Here I am. I'm stuck way up here and I can't get down." When his father saw where he was he was very upset. "What are you doing up there? Didn't I tell you not to climb any trees today?" Luke was very quiet as tears started running down his cheeks.

His father climbed up into the tree and very slowly and carefully freed him from the broken branch, held him close and cautiously carried him down to the ground.

"Luke, you disobeyed me and will have to be disciplined." Luke nodded his head. He knew he had disobeyed and deserved to be punished.

Then his father with a sigh of relief and a smile hugged Luke and assured him, "Luke, no matter what, I still love you and I always will. I'm so thankful that you didn't get hurt."

That's a good story, isn't it, Jeremiah? It's a reminder that God's love for us is like that. When we sin and do wrong we disappoint God and break His heart and He may have to discipline us but He never stops loving us no matter what.

Visual Aids:
Rubber bands (3 sizes), business
cards, newspaper, stack of mail

JESUS NEEDS ALL OF US

Jeremiah, I have something with me today that I know you have seen. {hold up small rubber band} This rubber band is so small that you would hardly ever notice it. It is like many Christians. You may hardly notice them for what they say and do but they are doing important jobs. Look what this tiny rubber band can do better than any other rubber band. {wrap it around business cards}

The little rubber band is actually able to do that better than this middle sized rubber band that I now hold in my hand.

However, this, too, is an important rubber band. It actually brings back some special memories for me. When I was a boy I had a paper route and delivered the Daily News six days a week while riding my bicycle. Each newspaper had been folded and wrapped with a rubber band just like this. {wrap around a newspaper}

The middle sized rubber band is like a pastor or a Sunday school teacher, used in a special and important way but still a rubber band.

Then there is a real big rubber band, thick and sturdy that goes around a big stack of mail. Our mail carrier uses rubber bands like these because the church usually gets so much mail. {wrap around a stack of mail} We could compare this to very talented and well known Christians like the Pope, Mother Teresa or Billy Graham. There are not very many rubber bands like this and we are certainly happy to have them but they are, nevertheless, still rubber bands.

You see, friends, like these rubber bands we come in various sizes and shapes with differing skills and abilities. God has made each of us unique with a special purpose in mind. There are some things you can do easily while other tasks seem so hard to do. But for someone else it is the opposite. What you find easy they find hard and what you find hard they find easy.

It is the way God made us. We are all a little different from each other. Yet each one of us is an important and loved member of God's family and He wants us to be the best that we can be with whatever He has given us to work with.

Like the rubber bands, we come in a variety of sizes with distinct purposes, but each of us is given an important job to do. You may never be famous but God is watching. He knows your name and what you are doing with what He gave you. Faithfully doing what God has equipped us to do is what really matters.

Visual Aids:

Small stuffed dog or puppet

LOVED JUST THE WAY YOU ARE

Jeremiah, I want you to meet a new friend. His name is Sparky. {pick up Sparky and hold him for entire story} For awhile Sparky was a very sad puppy because he had no home. His brothers and sisters had been adopted by happy pet owners so they all had new families.

Finally the day came when Sparky was adopted. A farmer had chosen him and Sparky was very excited. Now he would have a good home and be part of a family. Not only that but he would be living on a farm where there would be many other animals. He was certain that he would soon be having lots of fun with his new friends.

The next day he was up early, eager to meet the members of his new farm family.

The first one he met was huge. Sparky introduced himself and then asked "Who are you?" "Neigh." the giant answered, "I am a horse. The farmer really likes me because I am so strong. I can carry the farmer on my back and I can carry very heavy loads. What about you? Can you pull very heavy loads?" "No. I am just a puppy." "Humph!" snorted the horse and trotted off. Sparky was not very happy. This was not a good way to begin a new day. He rounded the corner and saw another huge animal, almost as big as the horse.

Once again Sparky opened up the conversation by announcing his name and then asking, "Who are you?" "I am a cow," she replied with a loud "moo" and continued, "The farmer really likes me because I give him fresh milk every morning. What about you? Can you give him fresh milk every morning?" Sparky looked up at her with big sad eyes and replied, "No, because I'm just a puppy." She shook her head, mooed loudly and walked away. Poor Sparky. This was turning out to be a miserable morning.

He was determined to find a friend somewhere and soon encountered a creature with feathers who was much smaller than the horse or cow. "Cluck, cluck, cluck," she said, and before Sparky would get in a word she cackled, "The farmer really likes me because I give him a fresh egg every morning. Can you do that?" "No," he murmured, "I am just a puppy." "Too bad," the chicken replied as she fluttered her feathers and entered the chicken coop. Poor Sparky. Now he was really unhappy, so much so that his heart was nearly breaking.

Coming down the pathway was another creature who seemed to be friendly. Sparky wagged his tail and said, "I'm Sparky, the puppy. Who are you?" "Bah, bah, bah," bellowed the proud critter, "I am a sheep and the farmer really likes me because I give him the wool off my back and he has used it to make a warm sweater for cold mornings. Can you give him something as nice as that?" "Well, no, I'm just a puppy." "Bah, bah, bah," Sparky heard as the sheep turned around and walked away.

Now Sparky was so distraught that tears started running down his cheeks. So with his head hanging low and his tail between his legs he slowly headed for home. That is when he met a very wise old dog who asked, "Puppy, what is the matter? Why are you looking so forlorn with tears in your eyes?" "Because all the other animals can do wonderful things for the farmer but I'm just a puppy and can't do anything."

"Oh, that's not true,," the wise old dog declared, "God made you special just the way you are. So you just be who you are and you'll bring joy to the farmer."

That sounded too good to be true but that evening when he saw the farmer coming in from the field after a hard day's work, Sparky started running toward him. His ears were flopping and his tail was wagging as he joyfully neared the farmer. The tired farmer stopped in his tracks and opened wide his arms. Sparky jumped right in and happily started licking him on the end of his nose. The farmer laughed, hugged Sparky and whispered, "Sparky, you make me so happy. I am so glad that you are part of my family. I love you just the way you are."

Jeremiah, that's a good story, isn't it? God made us all special and unique and there are some things others can do that I can't do but if I use whatever He has given me in ways that honor Him and bless others, He will smile and life will be very, very good.

LOST

Jeremiah, many years ago when our sons were quite young we took a wonderful vacation trip to Sweden. There we bought a new car, got a roadmap and planned to visit a relative that lived on a farm many miles from the city. We had driven a long ways and were just a few miles from our destination when we ran out of map. Now what? How would we ever find the farm with no more map?

We stopped at a farmhouse and I knocked on the door. A lady opened the door. I smiled and told her that we were lost and needed someone to give us directions. She looked confused, and shrugged her shoulders. I then realized that she spoke a different language so didn't understand what I had just said.

Fortunately, however, her college-age daughter appeared and could speak some English. We told her of our need. "Oh" she replied, "I know that family. I will give you directions." She then said something like this, "Go south along the main road for about 6 kilometers, turn right and go past a church. Then you will turn west and travel about 3 or 4 kilometers until you cross over a bridge. Now you are about half way there. Continue south on a gravel road for a short distance..." and on and on she went giving me more detailed instructions. I'm sure she saw the glazed look in my eyes and recognized that I was now mystified by what she was saying.

She stopped talking, smiled and remarked, "Why don't I get in my car and you follow me in your car and I will show you the way." That's what she did. She was our guide. We closely followed her and so we did not get lost. What a thoughtful, kind person she was. We thanked her from the bottom of our hearts.

What she did for us was a powerful reminder of what God has done for us. For many years He tried to help us find our way by sending prophets, teachers, and other leaders who attempted to tell us the right way to live our lives. So often, however, we got confused and lost or just didn't understand the whole story. We needed someone not just to tell us about the way but to show us the way. So God sent His son, Jesus, to lead us, guide us, and go with us. In fact, He said, "I am the way..." so if we follow Him we never again have to fear getting lost.

Visual Aids:
Child; 2 theater tickets; ticket taker

FOLLOW THE LEADER

Jeremiah, today we are going to need a volunteer to help us with our story. We need a helper who is a good follower. {select a child} Jonathan, thank you for helping us this morning. Your job is to follow me everywhere I go. We will soon discover how good a follower you are. {get up, move around room, change pace, etc.} Jonathan is still following. He is a good follower, isn't he?

Suppose I went out the door to my car, do you think he could still follow me? {children answer yes} Do you think he could follow me into a grocery store? {yes} What if I get into an elevator? {yes is still the answer}

Now watch closely. I am going to go to a movie theater and of course I'll give a ticket to the ticket taker. {hand her a ticket} I will go inside. Is Jonathan still following me? {ticket taker will not let him in} No? What happened? He wanted to keep following me but he couldn't because the ticket taker would not let him in without a ticket.

But wait a minute. I have a plan. I will buy a ticket for him. {hand over a ticket} I have paid the price for his ticket. Now the ticket taker is smiling and waving him in. Look, see the happy smile on Jonathan's face? He is still following. How wonderful!

Well friends, there are some times when we get stopped while following Jesus. Our sins, that is, disobedience, unkindness, not telling the truth, things like that get in the way of us following

Jesus. That's sad, but the good news is on the cross Jesus paid the penalty for all our sins. Now when life concludes we are able to follow Jesus right into heaven.

Jesus said, "I love you, I paid the price for you and now I've gone to heaven to prepare a place for you."

Thank you Jesus for this amazing gift, for paying the price for me. May I do a good job of following you for the rest of my life and pray I do it with a grateful heart.

Visual Aids:
Cloth sack,
Ball & Building Block

FILLED WITH THE HOLY SPIRIT

Jeremiah, a long, long time ago Pastor Eldon Weisheit, who is now in heaven, wrote a brief story about the Holy Spirit. Years ago when I read what he wrote I made some notes so I could remember it. My notes will help paraphrase what he said. Are you ready? Here comes the story.

All Christians, and that includes us, declare that we believe in the Holy Spirit. But it is hard for us to talk about a spirit, even the Holy Spirit because we can't see a spirit. But even though we cannot see the Spirit we know He is present when we see what He does. Let me show you what I mean.

See this sack. {sack with a ball in it} You can see nothing but the sack but you can tell that something is in it. Look. {twist sack tightly around the ball} Are you able to see the ball in the sack? Not really. You don't see the ball. You only see how the presence of the ball changes the shape of the sack.

By itself it has no shape. {hold empty sack} It takes on the shape of whatever is in it. {put children's building block in sack} See, the sack is now shaped like a building block.

In some ways we are like this empty sack. Left to ourselves we are weak and hollow and cannot serve God as we should. We need something or someone to give us strength and a purpose for living.

That is exactly what the Holy Spirit does even if I can't see him in you and you can't see him in me. But we can know the Holy Spirit is in each of us because we can see what He does.

We see the Holy Spirit the same way you saw the ball in the sack. When the Holy Spirit comes into us He brings Jesus into our lives and He changes everything about us just like the ball changed the shape of the sack. No longer is our life empty but is now filled with hope, love, faith, kindness and other beautiful traits. Even though we can't see the Holy spirit in each other we can see the beauty produced by the Holy Spirit living in us.

We are no longer empty sacks. Instead we are filled with the Spirit, living joyous lives of purpose and shaped daily by the presence of the Holy Spirit.

Visual Aids:
Saw, Razor Blade,
Knife, Hedge Clippers

EACH OF US IS CALLED TO SERVE

Jeremiah, if I asked you to bring me something with which to cut, what would you bring me? I suppose you could bring me hedge clippers {clippers} and that would be fine if I wanted to trim bushes in my backyard but what if I wanted to slice some carrots? Hedge clippers wouldn't work. So you bring me a knife. {knife} A knife will certainly cut many things but what if what I needed now was to shave? I sure wouldn't want to attempt to shave with a knife. What I need is a razor blade. {razor blade} Soon I plan to cut some wood. None of these cutters would work very well. Obviously what I would need would be a saw. {saw}

The point is this: in one sense they all do the same thing. They were made to be cutters. Yet it is clear to us that they all serve different purposes.

In the same way the Bible reminds us that we all have the same job to do because we are all followers of Jesus. We are all to use our talents, abilities, and gifts in God-pleasing ways but that doesn't mean we do exactly the same thing. Just as these tools all cut, so Christians all serve but not all in the same way.

Just think about some of the people you know, people with differing gifts, yet each serving the Lord. There are doctors, missionaries, preachers, lawyers, engineers, homemakers, teachers, moms, dads, grandparents, veterans, merchants, singers ... the list goes on and on. All don't have the same gifts but everyone has something to share.

Jeremiah, we haven't forgotten about children. Some might think they are too young to be serving Jesus but that is not true. Children serve by learning, singing, praying, helping others, obeying parents and teachers, sharing... the list goes on and on.

Friends, do you have anything to add to this list? How else might you serve ? {ask} Good. Good. Thank you.

There is another important point that we don't want to forget. That is whatever we do, however we serve, we do it with joy.

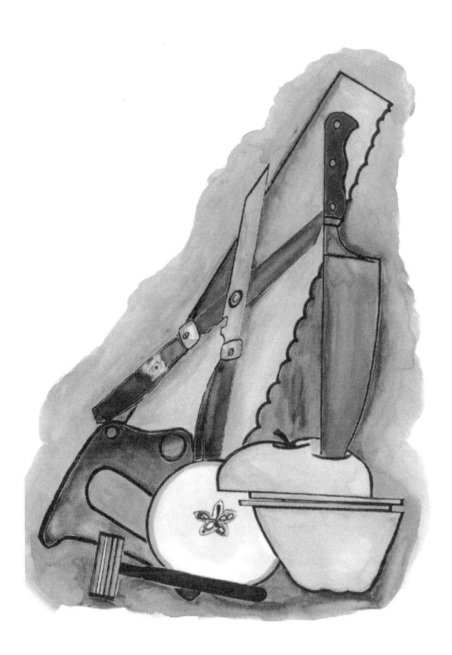

LIFE PROTECTORS

Jeremiah, in this box we have several life protectors. Each one is a symbol of something or someone that many trust as a life protector. I'm going to talk about each one of these and ask you to choose the one life protector that you want. {remove boxed items one at a time}

First we have a ten dollar bill. Ten dollars certainly can't protect you or save you but it is a symbol of money. If you were hungry it would buy food. If you were cold it would buy something warm to put on. If you were in a dangerous place it could buy you a ride to safety.

But there are some problems when counting on money to protect your life. It has its limitations. After all, you can't spend more than what you have and, more importantly, there are some things money cannot buy. If there is no food what good would money do? You couldn't eat it. The same thing is true with everything that you normally buy with money. Of course you can't buy life. Money may help you prolong life for a bit but it's not a lifesaver. People with lots of money die just as regularly as people without it.

For many the life protector is the family doctor. He is the symbol of all the medical help available to us. The lives of many have been saved by operations, vaccinations, drugs and other medications recommended by the doctor. A good doctor will most certainly help to improve the quality of life but even so his help is limited. Even healthy people eventually die.

Others will turn to the professions where men and women have been trained to protect and serve: police, firefighters and the military. Police will do whatever possible to prevent us from being hurt. Firefighters can be there to rescue us from the ravages of wildfire. Our military forces are on guard to halt any enemy from invading our country or mistreating our people. Nevertheless none of these protectors can guarantee that their actions will save our lives.

The cross is the fourth of our life protector symbols. It is a reminder that Jesus suffered, died and rose from the dead for us. Jesus is the only life protector with no limitations.

We are blessed to use all the life prolongers God has given us and thank Him for them. But Jesus is the ultimate life protector who will one day take us from this life to the next. We have an everlasting life protector when we have Jesus.

Jeremiah, we choose Jesus. There is no greater life protector.

Visual Aid:
Garden hoe

READY WHEN THE TIME COMES

Jeremiah, 800 years ago in the far off land of Assisi, there lived a remarkable man of God whose name was Francis. At one time he was very wealthy but he gave it all away and spent his lifetime helping the poor. The people respected him as a good man and a very wise person.

It is said that one day the elders of the city were discussing the following question, "If today was the last day you were going to be alive and you knew that for a fact, what would you do the rest of the day?" It was a very tough question. No one seemed to have a very good answer. Then someone suggested that Francis be asked that question. They knew that he was very wise and always had good answers for their questions.

Two of them, Luke and Jonathan, were selected to represent the group and were sent on their way to visit Francis.

As they approached Francis they noted that he was outside his humble little home hoeing his garden. "Excuse me, sir," they said, "We have a question to ask you. The city elders have been discussing this question all day and cannot come up with a satisfactory answer. We know that you are a wise man of God and so we have been sent to ask it of you. Here is the question: 'Francis, if today was the last day of your life and you knew that for certain, what would you do the rest of the day?" Francis smiled, looked at the men who were waiting breathlessly for his answer and calmly replied, "Gentlemen, I would finish hoeing my garden."

It was such a simple answer to their question but also such a wonderful answer. Francis was telling them that he would change nothing. He would continue doing what he was doing. He would not have to panic, run to church, fall on his knees and beg God to forgive him and save him. He had already done that and knew that Christ had paid the penalty for his sins on the cross and he was forgiven. Heaven's gates would be open for him whenever his final day arrived.

Francis also knew that he would not have to frantically seek out someone he had hurt or offended and try to make it right. He had already done that. He was daily living his life in a right relationship with God and with his neighbors.

What a marvelous example he has set for us! It should also be our goal that when our final day comes God will find us "hoeing our garden!" That is, ready and prepared, in a good relationship with God and our neighbor.

Visual Aids:
Oyster shell; pearl

GOOD TROUBLES

Jeremiah, there is an old, old parable about an oyster and a pearl. It is a great story about how troubles can sometimes turn into blessings.

Here is the story: There once was an oyster who lived in a shell like this. {show shell} He lived deep in the ocean and, much like a turtle, a shell was his home. Occasionally he would open his shell to take in water and tiny objects for his food. He was usually able to push out anything not good for food.

One day, however, a small grain of sand got under the shell. Ouch! It soon was causing pain and the oyster tried to get rid of it. But no matter what he did he could not shake the intruder out of his shell. He decided to learn to live with his trouble.

Gradually over the months that followed the invader was coated over and over again with a special silky substance from the oyster. This helped keep it from hurting so much. The grain of sand grew bigger until one day it became a beautiful pearl. What had started as trouble later resulted in a marvelous and expensive jewel. {show pearl}

Sometimes God uses our troubles to make pearls. For example, a boy named Finn was sick for a long time and forced to stay in bed. For many that would have been a sad and wasted time filled with disappointment. But Finn, much to his credit, spent many hours reading some great books. He learned a lot during that time of sickness and was soon one of the best students in his class. He was able to turn his troubles into pearls.

That is a wonderful lesson for all of us. Remember, even when bad things happen and trouble comes, God does not stop loving us but has a way of bringing some good out of that which first appeared to be only bad.

What a great God we have!

Visual Aid:

Long stem rose with a thorn

MOTHER

Jeremiah, one of the commandments of Scripture is to honor our father and our mother. With that thought in mind I would like to celebrate our mothers by comparing a mother to a rose.

Take a good look at it. {hold up rose} Almost everyone thinks that a rose is pretty and just about everyone I know thinks their mother is quite pretty, too. Isn't that right Jeremiah? I knew that you would agree and nod your head.

The second reason why a rose reminds me of mother is that it smells so good. I remember as a small boy coming into the kitchen when my mother was baking chocolate chip cookies. I'd bury my nose in her apron and sigh, "Mama, you smell so good. Just like a chocolate chip cookie."

The third reason why a rose reminds me of mother is that it has such soft and tender petals. There are some days when you're not feeling so good, maybe a bit disappointed or sad. You crawl up into Mother's lap. It is a soothing and peaceful place to be as she wraps her arms around you. Soon everything is better.

There is one more reason why a rose reminds me of mother and this may surprise you. Do you see down here on the stem there is a sticker? Ouch! A thorn like this can hurt. Why in the world would this remind me of mother? Here's why. A godly mother will discipline her children when they disobey because she deeply cares for them and wants them to grow up to be honest, good and kind. Discipline hurts but only for a little while. It is done as an act of love by a mother who is training her children to be the best they can be.

So how do you say thanks to a wonderful mother? Well, of course, you could give her a beautiful rose. I'm sure she would like that but even a better idea would be to whisper in her ear, "I love you and I'm so glad that you're my mom," and then give her a big hug.

A godly mother has no greater joy or reward than knowing that her children are following Jesus.

FAITH LIKE A MUSTARD SEED

Jeremiah, have you ever seen a mustard seed? I have one here and I am holding it right up in front of your face. Yet it is so very tiny that you can hardly see it. It is the smallest seed that I have ever seen. Even though it is so very very small when it is planted in the ground it grows so big that birds can sit in its branches. Some might even build their nests in it. I have been told that some of these tiny mustard seeds can produce a plant that grows over ten feet high! That is truly amazing.

Jesus once told a parable about a mustard seed in which He said to his disciples, "If you have faith even if it is as small as a mustard seed you will be able to do astonishing things."

I heard a story that I think will help all of us better understand what Jesus meant when He talked about having faith like a mustard seed.

It was about a young girl, Emma, who got lost in the woods on a farm not far from her home. The farmer who owned the land joined a search team that went looking for her. He heard what sounded like a child's voice. He stopped, quietly listening. Then he called out, "Emma, Emma, is that you?" A happy voice responded, "Here I am. I was waiting for you. I knew you would find me."

The farmer was perplexed. "You were waiting for me? What made you think that I was coming?"

"I was praying that you would," she said.

"You were praying?" the farmer asked, "when I first heard you, you were just saying the alphabet A B C D E F G ... it didn't sound like praying. What was that all about?"

She smiled and then said simply, "I wasn't sure how to pray or what to say, so I just decided to pray the letters of the alphabet and let God put them together the way He wanted them. He knew I was lost and He knew what I was thinking and what I needed most."

Emma had faith, perhaps no bigger than a mustard seed, but it was enough. Her prayer of faith was answered in a wonderful way and she soon was home again with her family.

Visual Aids:
Flashlight;
Batteries

HOLY SPIRIT

Jeremiah, I remember one night we had a power outage. All our electricity went off which meant that all our lights went dark. I was not that concerned though since I knew that we had a flashlight in our garage. I had not used it for a long time and had forgotten where I put it. At last, to my relief, I found it. But guess what? It didn't work. The old batteries were dead.

That experience reminded me of a children's story I told one time about a flashlight. Flashlights can be very useful. They can be used to find our way in the dark and keep us from stumbling.

The flashlight I'm holding now looks like it could be quite helpful. The switch works fine and the bulb is not burnt out but it has no batteries so it is of little value. What do batteries do? They furnish the power.

In some ways Christians are like flashlights. Jesus told his disciples, "You are the light of the world." He was saying that He wants us to be the kind of people that make the darkness go away, the darkness of hopelessness, unhappiness and despair. He wants us to be His flashlights.

The flashlight cannot do its job without good batteries. {put them in} YES! Now the flashlight has its power source and is able to shine brightly.

Where do we get our power source? Jesus said, "You shall receive power from the Holy Spirit." When that happens your light will shine in marvelous ways.

How does the Holy Spirit come? He often comes to us and speaks to us through prayer, the Bible, our Sunday School teachers, and our parents. After we have received the Holy Spirit we have power to become Jesus' flashlight in a dark world.

Remember the happy song, "This little light of mine, I'm gonna let it shine, let it shine, let it shine..."

The Holy spirit furnishes the power and we become God's flashlights.

Visual Aid:

Baking chocolate

KNOW YOUR ENEMY

Jeremiah, many, many years ago, perhaps as long as fifty years ago, I remember reading a book of short stories written by Pastor Wesley Runk. Most of the stories have long been forgotten but one about "wolves in sheep's clothing" still stands out in my memory.

The story went something like this: There are some people who cannot be trusted. They are like wolves in sheep's clothing. Do you know what a wolf looks like? {someone describe a wolf} Now can you tell me what sheep's clothing looks like? {describe} Now I think you can imagine what a wolf in sheep's clothing looks like. The crafty wolves did this so they could sneak up on the sheep and eat them.

Jesus said that we have to be careful about certain kinds of deceitful people who want us to listen to them, follow them and do what they say. On the outside they may look just fine but they teach things which are not true and are contrary to the Bible. They sometimes are very clever and what they say sounds good and looks good but it can lead to heartache and misery.

Let me give you an example. I brought some delicious-looking chocolate with me today. It is real chocolate, brown and shaped like candy that most of us would enjoy. If you'd like some I'll give you a piece to eat, but let me warn you, you're not going to like it. {by now there is always someone who will tell you that they would like it} So you think it looks tasty and you'd like some. OK, I'll give you some. {do it} You may eat it right now. How do you like it? {by now the volunteer is probably looking sick and trying to spit it out}

"What? You don't like this chocolate? But it looks so good." It's like a wolf in sheep's clothing. It is called "Baker's Chocolate" and tastes very bitter and is used only in baking.

I did this to show you that sometimes people teach things that are not in the Bible but they make it look as good as this piece of chocolate.

Remember: if what is taught is different from what is in the Bible we must stay away from it.

Visual Aids:
Photo poster of
lost dog–reward

JOY WHEN THE LOST IS FOUND

Jeremiah, as I walk around our neighborhood, I sometimes see signs like this one. {hold up lost dog sign} It says, "Lost Dog. Our little dog, Winnie, has been missing since January 10. We love Winnie very much and we want him back. If you find Winnie, please call us at 829-4766. Reward."

I always feel sad when I see a poster like this. I can imagine the family watching and hoping that their beloved pet will be found. There would be a sense of excitement every time the phone would ring. It might be a call from someone who has found Winnie.

I would think there might also be a fear that their little dog had been run over by a car. Or, and this would be quite possible in our neighborhood, a coyote ate him up.

Have you ever lost something that was very precious to you? How did you feel? Have you ever found something that you had lost? If so, do you remember how good you felt when you found it?

One of the best known stories that Jesus told is about a man who lost something that was very precious to him. The story also told of his great joy when that which he had lost was found. This is that famous story that Jesus told.

A man had two sons. The younger son demanded that his father give him his share of his inheritance and give it to him now. His demand showed a total lack of love and respect for his father. Nevertheless, the father gave it to him. The young man immediately left home and soon spent all his money in wild and foolish ways. In the meantime the father was brokenhearted. He had lost his son.

Before long everything the son had been given was wasted and gone. He had no job, no food, no friends, no place to stay. He was desperate. He finally got a part-time job feeding pigs. Can you believe it? He was living in a pig sty with a bunch of noisy, dirty pigs. He was so hungry that even the slop the pigs were eating looked good to him.

Finally he came to his senses. "I'm going home," he said to himself, "and will beg my father to give me a job as one of his hired servants." Dirty, smelly and barefoot he headed for home.

The young man's father was waiting and hoping that his boy would come home. Even though he had broken his father's heart, his father had never stopped loving him. When he saw his son coming he ran to meet him. He wrapped his arms around him, hugged him and kissed him.

The father was so happy to see his son that he gave him a robe, some shoes and placed a priceless family ring on his finger.

"Prepare a feast!" he shouted, "my son was lost but now is found."

Jesus told this story to show the kind of forgiving love God has for us and all his children. When one of God's children strays from home it breaks His heart, but He always welcomes him with open arms when he comes home.

How wonderful to be loved like that.

CHOICES

Jeremiah, don't you get excited when the mail comes and there is a letter for you? Of course, I think we all like to receive mail. For example, I know that you would be happy to get a letter like this. {hold up invitation} Here is what it says: "You are invited to my birthday party at my house this Saturday at 2:00 PM ." Then it is signed, "with love, your friend, Emma."

You are delighted and ready to say yes when you notice that you have another letter. {pick up second invitation} This, too, is an invitation to a birthday party next Saturday at 2:00 PM. It is from your friend, Luke. Now you have a problem. You're really happy to be invited to these parties but why do they have to be at the same time? You are going to have to make a choice. You can't be two places at the same time.

Jesus told a parable, a story, about people who had a choice to make. A man invited many friends to a banquet. One of his friends thought: do I go to a banquet or check out the new farm that I bought? Another man thought: do I go to the banquet or see what kind of a deal I got on the animals I just bought? And yet another person has to make a choice: do I go to the banquet or spend a pleasant, quiet evening at home with my wife? In each case a choice was made. Each selected what was most important to him.

Jesus told this parable because He knows that each of us has choices to make every day. Play a video game, read a book, or go play ball. We can't do everything at the same time so we have to make choices. The choices we make indicate what we think is most important.

Here is another example. It is Sunday morning and you are getting ready for Sunday School when your soccer coach calls and invites you to come to the playing field where a photographer is waiting to take the team photo. (That actually happened to us many years ago.) Your choice shows what is most important to you.

Every day we make choices. So did Jesus. He chose to go to the cross to pay the penalty for your sins. He made that choice because He loves you so much.

Think about His love for you as you make choices every day.

Visual Aids:

Your hand

FIVE FINGER PRAYER

Do you know, Jeremiah, there are times when I start to pray and then I just can't think of anything to say. I'm quite sure that happens to a lot of people.

Somebody whose name unfortunately I don't remember, said that when she can't think of anything to say in her prayers she will then use what she called her "Five Finger Prayer."

Here is what she does. She puts her hands together in front of her and keeps her eyes open so she can see her hands. When you do that you will notice that you nearest finger is your thumb. Since it is closest to you, your thumb reminds you to pray for those that are closest to you. Pray for your parents, your grandparents, and your brothers and sisters.

The next finger is called your index finger. It is used for pointing. The finger can remind you to pray for those that are pointing you in the right direction. Pray for your pastor, Sunday School teachers, and for all those who set good examples for you.

The next finger is the tallest of all your fingers. This reminds you to pray for your leaders. Pray for the president of our country, for the mayor of your town and for the principal of your school.

The fourth finger is called the ring finger. Did you know that this is the weakest finger you have? Just ask anyone who plays the piano and they will tell you that this is true. Let the finger remind you to pray for the weak. the poor, the homeless, the sick, orphans and those that have no one to love them.

The next finger is the smallest finger. Jesus said, "Unless you become like a little child you have no place in my kingdom." So you'll want to be humble and trusting like a small child and it will be your little finger that will remind you of these words of Jesus as you pray for yourself.

So the next time you are talking to God and can't think of anything to pray let the "Five Finger Prayer" help you.

Visual Aids:

10 pennies for each child

TITHING: OUR GIFT TO GOD

Jeremiah, do you see what I have today? It is a sack full of pennies. Let's look at one very closely. See, here is our greatest president, Abraham Lincoln, and right below him the date when the coin was minted. We also see the word "liberty" and the motto, "in God we trust."

The back has a picture of the Lincoln Memorial, the words "United States of America" and "one cent." Then a Latin phrase "E Pluribus Unum" which means "from many, one."

All that on a penny which has almost no worth today. About all we can do with a penny is pay sales tax on a purchase or if we save enough of them we may be able to buy something worthwhile. But today we are going to use a penny to help us learn a very important lesson.

I will be God's helper today and in His name I will give each of you ten pennies. I hope that you will place at least one of your ten pennies in the offering this week. You can keep the other nine: it's a free gift, but I would hope you would use them in ways that you know are God-pleasing.

OK. Now let's get back to the penny that I have asked you to put in the offering. We call this tithing. It means giving back one in ten.

Jeremiah, I know that this is hard for our friends to grasp now but as they grow older it will become clearer. In the meantime we want them to know how important it is to always share what we have received.

Today our friends are learning to share their pennies. Some day, after they have grown up, they will share their dollars. So we learn to tithe when we are young and trust that we will all continue to do this as we grow older.

God's word teaches that tithing is a wonderful way for us to share equally what God has given us. It is a great way to say thank you to God for all His blessings.

A tithe is God's way: giving one out of ten. I hope that each time we look at this little brown coin we'll remember the meaning of tithing.

Visual Aids:

Photo of orangutang; large "check"

THANKSGIVING

Jeremiah, some years ago the zookeeper made a visit to our school. He was quite concerned that the animals at the zoo would all be well fed and cared for. However, they had encountered some financial problems. They did not have enough money to properly care for all the animals.

It was decided that the zookeeper would visit various schools and other organizations to encourage groups to "adopt" a zoo animal; that is, to provide money to take care of the needs of a specific animal. So that is what he did. The children in our school thought this would be a wonderful idea. They could choose any animal in the entire zoo and then join with their parents and teachers in a fundraiser. Everyone agreed that this would be a very good cause and something they wanted to do. Guess what animal they chose to adopt? Here he is. {hold up picture of orangutang} A huge orangutang!

They excitedly went to work and in no time at all they had raised enough money to take care of their adopted friend. A big check was made out to the zoo. {hold up enlarged check} Soon the children, their teachers and some parents traveled to the zoo to meet their orangutang friend, present the check and have a photo taken. They were standing near the enclosure where their teacher was holding the check way up in the air so the photographer could get a good picture.

Suddenly the orangutang reached out his hand and somehow managed to grab the check. He immediately crumpled it up {crumple up the check}, put it in his mouth, chewed on it, spit it out and stomped on it, picked it up and threw it away. The startled children watched with eyes very wide open wondering what had happened. They were shocked. What a terrible, ungrateful response to a gift.

Boys and girls, God has "adopted" us as his precious children and has provided us with an abundance of gifts, everything we need. Families, food, friends and on and on it goes, so many blessings we can't even number them all. God forbid that we should ever treat our blessings like the ungrateful orangutang did. May all of us always have grateful hearts.

HOW TO HANDLE WORRY

Jeremiah, there is a story that I've told many, many times. It is a reminder on how to handle worry. I don't remember if it is a tale that I heard from someone else or did it come out of my head? Oh well, I won't worry about it. I'll just retell it.

Jeremiah, I am upset, filled with worries. Christmas is coming soon and I have so much to do to get ready and I am running out of time. I haven't even sent out a single Christmas card yet. Worry, worry, worry. I desperately need a worry pill. {swallow one} Oh, good, good. Now that irksome thought has been removed.

Oh, no, woe is me. Here comes another possible problem. So many people catch colds or the flu this time of year. What if I get sick? I wouldn't be able to get any Christmas shopping done. Worry, worry, worry.{swallow pill} Oh, good. Another troubling thought has been erased.

Oh no, more frightening thoughts. We have family members coming soon to celebrate Christmas with us. We want everything to be really nice when they arrive. All our holiday decorations are still tucked away in boxes and I don't know where I'll ever find the time to put them all up. Worry, worry, worry. {swallow pill} I'm so grateful for worry pills. Now those fearful thoughts won't bother me anymore.

Oh, no, no, no. Really big aggravation coming into my mind. It is a sea of trouble that returns every year. It is my biggest worry.

What am I going to get my wife for Christmas? Worry, worry, worry .{swallow another worry pill} Whew! Sometimes I even worry that I might run out of worry pills.

I started thinking how wonderful it would be if just one pill could be taken that would end all of my worries. Maybe if I had just one really big pill instead of all these little ones I would never worry again.

{PAUSE} Jeremiah, I have been so silly. There is no such thing as "worry pills." What I have been eating is simply small pieces of candy and they can do nothing to eliminate worry. But, thanks be to God, we don't need worry pills. He has given us something far better. Jesus said, "Bring all your worries and anxieties to me and I will get rid of all of them. I'll do it because I love you."

That wonderful promise from Jesus is so much better than worry pills.

Visual Aids:
Books, Dumbbells,
Trophy, Dollars

HOW TO GET TO HEAVEN

Jeremiah, I think everyone wants to go to heaven some day but some people have some very strange ideas on how to do that. For example, there are those who believe that heaven has been prepared for smart people, those with all the right answers,{hold up several books} those who get high marks on their exams and have several degrees after their name. Of course, it is always a good idea to study hard, do the best we can, and get a good education. However, that is not going to get us into heaven.

Others believe heaven has been prepared for those that are strong. {hold up dumbbells} Of course, it is always wise to take good care of our bodies, eat the right foods and get plenty of exercise, but we're never going to get into heaven on our own strength.

Someone I know received this trophy {hold up trophy} because he was selected as the most valuable player on his team. People cheer for him and want his autograph. He is very popular and seems to be a nice person but not even a sackful of trophies will get him into heaven.

Then there are some people who have lots of money {hold up a handful of dollars} and throughout their lifetime have always been able to buy just about anything they wanted. Some live their lives in such a way that is seems they think they can even buy a ticket to heaven. Money can surely be a blessing if used in God-honoring ways but it will not open heaven's gates.

Jesus said, "I go to prepare a place for you.." and then He went to the cross where He paid the price for us that will open heaven's doors. Jesus is the way and it is only in following Him that we will find our way to heaven.

Visual Aid:
New inflated ball

LIFE'S PURPOSE

Jeremiah, do you see what I have today? It is a terrific new ball that my neighbor gave me. It is such a special gift that I'm going to display it where all my friends can see it. It is going right here on top of this table. {place ball on table} There. That is the proper place for it. Now I'm going to call my friend Andrew and invite him to come over and see this marvelous gift.

Andrew soon arrives and I excitedly point out to him my brand new ball on exhibition on my table. I invite Andrew to sit down on the floor beside me as I gaze at the ball with a look of wonderment on my face. Andrew is very puzzled by all this. Then he sees me pick up the ball, carefully polish it with my handkerchief, and then with a satisfied expression, lovingly place it back on the table. Time goes by and we do nothing but sit and observe the ball.

Jeremiah, this would not be any fun at all, would it? No, it would be foolish. A fabulous ball like this was not made to sit on a table for people to look at. The manufacturer made it for boys and girls to play with it. The purpose of a ball like this is to be bounced, thrown, caught, kicked, an outside toy to bring enjoyment to all who play with it. That is its purpose.

Well, Jeremiah, there are lots of people who don't know why God made them. They have yet to figure out what their purpose is. They may try something for awhile and then switch to something else but nothing brings much satisfaction. They are left feeling empty. The days go by stretching into months and then years but no real purpose is found and so their hearts are restless and unsatisfied.

All of that can change when we recognize that God made each of us with a specific purpose in mind. This is what Jesus said: we have been placed here to love God and to love each other. When we discover that all of life becomes more exciting and is filled with meaning. Of course, we are all made a little differently so how we demonstrate that love may be unique for each of us. Nevertheless, knowing our purpose and then doing it can turn our entire existence into a joyful life of value and significance.

Visual Aids:
Raw egg; ball; pan

THE RIGHT WAY

Jeremiah, many years ago when I was a pastor in Ohio I heard a very interesting story told by Pastor Wesley Runk. It was about an egg and a ball and the problems they caused for someone who thought he didn't have to follow the rules.

We all have learned that there is a right way and a wrong way to do just about everything. For example, here is an egg and here is a ball. Now one of these you are to cook and eat and one of these you are to bounce. But there are always those who think that the rules don't apply to them. They think that they can do anything they want to do. Who cares about the rules? They think if they want to bounce the egg and eat the ball then that is what they are going to do.

And so someone with that attitude took the egg and announced, "I don't believe in foolish rules. I want to do things my own way so if I want to bounce the egg and cook and eat this ball then that is exactly what I am going to do."

With a look of defiance on his face he held the egg high over the pan {do it} and dropped it. Yikes! It splattered all over and made a terrible mess. He learned the hard way that the rules were made for him, too.

Jeremiah, when God made the world He set up certain laws that were intended to be obeyed by all of us. When we try to follow them all of life is better for us. If we think that we don't need to listen to God's rules we end up doing foolish things and we are filled with regrets.

May God help us to resist the temptation to do something that is contrary to God's plan. His rules are given to us because He loves us and doesn't want us to make a mess out of our lives.

There is a right way and a wrong way to do just about everything. It is always best to follow God's rules and do it God's way.

Visual Aid:
Book with a cover
from another book

CAN'T TELL A BOOK BY ITS COVER

Jeremiah, as you can plainly see, today I have a rather large book. I thought it might be of interest to our friends. Can anybody tell me the name of the book? {read title} That's right. The name of the book is "One Hundred and One Famous Hymns." It is a book about some of our most beloved hymns, who wrote them and why. It sounds interesting. Some of these stories are going to bring us some surprises.

Let's open the book and take a look at one of the stories. Hey! This book isn't about hymns. In fact I don't see anything here about a single song. All I see are pictures of dogs. This book is not about hymns at all. It's a book about caring for dogs.

How can this be? The cover clearly states "One Hundred and One Famous Hymns" yet on the inside it is all about raising dogs. Can someone help me figure out how this could have happened?

What? It had the wrong cover? Of course. That solves the problem. All along we believed the book was about hymns because that's what the cover said. Looking only at the cover is what misled us.

People can be like books with covers. You may think that you know all about them because of their appearance. But you only see how they look on the outside. You may discover after you really get to know them that your first impression-when you could only see the outside-is different from whom they really are.

That is why God always looks on the inside, right into the heart. He knows that what is on the inside is the real you and that is much more valuable than what appears on the outside.

Next time you're meeting some new people remember that you can't always tell a book by its cover. It will help you to remember that what you discover on the inside is far more important than what you can see on the outside.

Visual Aid:

Mother Goose story book

or similar book

PEOPLE OF THE LAST CHAPTER

Jeremiah, this is a very special storybook. Look. {hold up book} I'm sure most of our friends know these stories. They are fun to hear because they have happy endings.

You can be sad when Cinderella has to stay home while her stepmother and stepsisters go to the Prince's Ball (which is a really fancy dance party). But you know that your sadness will soon turn to gladness because you recall that she will go to the Ball, will lose her glass slipper but the Prince will fall in love with her, find her and they will live happily ever after.

When Red Riding Hood takes a basket of goodies to her sick grandmother and instead meets the Big Bad Wolf, it can be kind of scary but then you remember that the woodsman will come to Red Riding Hood's rescue and she is not going to be harmed. The story has a happy ending.

Snow White is hated by the Queen because her magic mirror said that Snow White was prettier than she was. In a furious rage the Evil Queen gives Snow White a poisoned apple and makes her fall into a deep sleep. The Evil Queen thinks Snow White is dead but the handsome prince finds her, she is revived and we all smile because of the happy ending.

Followers of Jesus feel the same way about life. We've read the story and although there are some sad parts we know that the story has a happy ending.

St. Paul wrote in the Bible these words of God, "All things work together for good to those who love the Lord." We know that no matter what happens Jesus has won the greatest battle of all. He has conquered death and the grave and has given hope and meaning to our lives. Because He won, we His children, will win, too.

We have read the last chapter. We know that the story has a a happy ending. Knowing how the story ends gives us a sense of peace and joy and makes every day a good day.

Visual Aids:
Football & Doll

HIS GREATEST CATCH

Jeremiah, as you know many of us enjoy the game of football. So today I'm going to tell our friends a football story and what makes it so exciting is that it is true. That's right, it actually happened.

A football player in Florida, James Harris, was a great receiver. That means that he could catch almost any ball thrown anywhere near him. After awhile he was given the nickname "Big Hands Harris."

It was the final game of the season. The score was tied. "Big Hands" team had the ball with only one more minute to play. The hometown fans were on their feet shouting, "Throw it to Big Hands". That is exactly what happened. The quarterback hurled the ball into the end zone. Big Hands made a leaping catch for a touchdown. {toss and catch football} The crowd gave out a thunderous roar. The hometown team had won the game.

The next day the local newspaper had a photo of Big Hands making his spectacular catch. The caption read, "Big Hands' Greatest Catch". But, do you know what, that wasn't to be his greatest catch.

A few weeks later Big Hands was out jogging one evening when he smelled smoke. He was alarmed. Something was wrong. Then he saw, off in the distance, a house engulfed in flames. It seemed like the entire downstairs was ablaze. Fire fighters were coming but they weren't there yet. As he got closer he heard a woman screaming, "Help me! Help me!" She was upstairs in that burning house, leaning out a window and holding a baby. The fire was getting closer and in desperation she begged, "Help!" and then dropped the baby out the window right into the waiting hands of Big Hands Harris. {catch tossed doll} He caught the baby so gently that she wasn't even hurt, not even a little bit.

The next day the newspaper printed two pictures of Big Hands on the front page. In the first photo he was holding a football. The caption read, "His greatest catch? No". Then the second photo, holding the rescued baby, read, "His greatest catch".

Well, Jeremiah, I enjoy watching football games and seeing great catches but there really is no greater joy then knowing that you have helped another person, and that you have made a positive difference in their life.

SPECIAL OCCASIONS

GETTING READY FOR JESUS

Jeremiah, it happens in nearly every home as Christmas approaches. It happened in Finn's home. He woke up one morning and discovered that just about everyone in the family was up and working. There was vacuuming, dusting, cleaning; even some furniture was being moved. Finn's mother told him to pick up all his toys and to clean his room. She said she wanted his room to be "clean as a whistle."

He didn't have to ask why because he knew why. Grandpa and Grandma were coming for the holidays and his parents wanted everything to look nice and ready for their visit. After all, that is the way to make guests feel welcome. Have everything as "spic and span" as possible before they arrive in order for everyone to enjoy their visit and spend relaxing time with each other.

Jesus told us that He would soon be coming. We surely want to be ready for His arrival. The preparation we do for his coming is not done with a broom or vacuum cleaner-of course not. The cleaning we need to do is to get rid of the muck and dirt in our hearts so Jesus will feel welcome there. This is done when we repent; that is, we confess to Jesus that we are sorry for that which we have done or left undone that made Him sad. It happens when we ask for strength and courage to do only that which will put a smile on His face.

We don't know when He is coming and so we want to be prepared whenever that day arrives. This means that we want to live our lives every day in such a way that we'll be ready whenever He comes. There will be no need to panic or frantically try to make some last minute changes. Simply living each day at peace with God, in a right relationship with others, striving to love as we have been loved. Then, whenever that day arrives it will be a glad and joyous time because we are ready to meet Jesus face to face.

Jeremiah, we want to express our appreciation to Dr. Harold Uhl for sharing this story with us. He is a wonderful story teller and we thank God for him.

Visual Aids:

Doll in a box

CHRISTMAS IS COMING

Jeremiah, we are fast approaching one of the happiest times of the year. What do you think that is? Christmas! Of course. People are starting to put up decorations, lights, trees and beautiful wreaths. Delightful Christmas carols are floating through the airways, nativity scenes are appearing in a variety of places and many children are happily joining others in rehearsals getting ready for the annual Sunday School Christmas pageant.

Something else is also starting to arrive, many beautifully wrapped packages containing wonderful surprises. I have a gift package that contains something that reminds us of the real meaning of Christmas. {hold up package} What do you think is in the package? Santa Claus stocking cap? No. A snowman? No. A little plastic reindeer? No.

Let's open it and see what it is that reminds us of Christmas. {open box and remove doll} A baby! Why would a baby remind us of Christmas? You're right. We celebrate Christmas because it was on this day that the baby Jesus was born. It is Jesus' birthday.

Christmas is also a time for the giving and receiving of gifts. That is fine. It is one way to show family and friends that we care about them. But remember what we said earlier: Christmas is Jesus' birthday so what are you planning to give Him on his special day?

I believe I know what you are thinking. You are thinking how is it possible to actually give Jesus a Christmas present? Jesus himself answered that question when He said that anything you do for someone who is poor, weak, lonely, helpless or in need you've done it for Him.

Jeremiah, that is exciting news, isn't it? When we bring in our Christmas gifts for the poor children in Mexico it is our way of giving a gift to Jesus.

I think I can already hear {cup your ear} Jesus saying thank you.

Visual Aids:

Apple, Knife

THE BETHLEHEM STAR

Jeremiah, we just celebrated Christmas and what a happy time we all had. Because it was Jesus' birthday we sang, "Happy Birthday, dear Jesus." For most of us it is our favorite time of the year.

I'm going to ask you some questions to see how much you remember of the Christmas story. Are you ready?

Here is the first question, "Who told Mary and Joseph where to find the stable where the baby would be born? The innkeeper, of course. That was a good answer. Next question, who were the first ones to announce the birth of the baby Jesus? The angels. You're right again. Another question, who were the first people to visit the newborn King? The shepherds. So far you've had the right answers for all my questions. Here is my final question, What was the sign that led the wise men to find the Savior? A star. I'm so very glad that you know this story so well.

It seems that the Wise Men were the only ones who noticed the star and followed it. That's why we call them WISE. No one else paid any attention to the star or maybe it was hidden from them.

Speaking of hidden stars I know a special place where God has hidden a star. Right here in the center of this apple. {hold up the apple} That is why you will sometimes see an apple in paintings of Jesus and His mother. That is why when we put up our

Christmas tree we always include an apple somewhere in our decorations. We do this because we know an apple hides a star.

Sometimes we cut an apple through the top and bottom but today we are going to cut it through the middle, like cutting through the equator of the world. {cut apple} Look closely, what do you see? Yes, a star! A wonderful reminder of the story of Christmas hidden in an apple.

I hope and pray that this will remind us to try to be wise like the wise men of the Christmas story who knew that nothing was more important than finding Jesus.

Visual Aids:
Beautifully wrapped
package & brown paper bag

CHRISTMAS GIFT

Jeremiah, if these two packages were under your Christmas tree and you could choose one, which would you take? Look how beautifully wrapped this one is. But if you chose it you would be disappointed. {unwrap} See, it is an empty box wrapped to look like a gift. It was used only for display purposes and is of no value.

This other package has a real gift. Look what is here: a $100 gift certificate! You could take it to the store and get whatever you wanted. Wow! What a neat gift. If you received a really nice gift like this you wouldn't care how it was wrapped. It is the gift that counts, not the package it comes in.

This is also true of God's gift to us. In the Christmas story the angel told the shepherds that they would find the baby Jesus wrapped in swaddling cloths. He wouldn't be wearing fancy baby clothes; instead he would be wrapped in a plain white towel which is what swaddling cloths are. The angel also said that he would be lying in a manger. No expensive crib for this baby. Instead, he would be in a makeshift animal food trough. Ugh! That was like a special present in a plain brown paper bag.

But Jesus was such a precious gift that a store-bought gown and a jewel-studded crib were not needed for God's ultimate gift to us.

On that first Christmas God gave us the greatest gift ever given: His own son. So what can we give him in return? What does He want more than anything else? He wants our love. That is the greatest gift that we can give Him.

Wait just a minute! Jeremiah has asked me a very good question. He wants to know what we can do to show Jesus how much we love Him. Jeremiah, Jesus answered that question when He said, "when you do it unto the least of my brothers and sisters, you've done it unto me."

When we show kindness and love to the weak and the poor, Jesus smiles and says, "Thank you." It is like we did it for him.

A FEW DAYS AFTER CHRISTMAS

Jeremiah, a minister in a church in Alabama would sometimes begin his children's sermon with a question. Here is a question that Pastor Eldon Weisheit asked the Sunday after Christmas. Are you ready? OK. "What did you get for Christmas last year?" He wasn't asking them what they had received just a few days ago. No, he wanted to know if they could remember Christmas gifts that they were given over a year ago.

That was a tough question. I'm not sure that I could answer it. I would have to give it some careful thought. Nevertheless I think he asked a very good question. We can tell how much you appreciated your past gifts by how well you remembered what you did with them. To show you how this works I'll tell you about some of my past gifts.

I opened a package from my cousin who was serving in the Air Force in Thailand. Here it is. {money clip} It was a unique gift but I've never used it. It has been sitting in my dresser drawer for a year.

This necktie {necktie} was a gift to me from a Korean pastor. It is a very nice-looking tie and I've worn it four or five times.

This wallet {wallet} was a present from one of my sons. Guess what? I use it every day. It carries my driver's license, credit cards and some cash. Because it holds my identification I won't leave home without it.

Now about the Christmas gifts you received last year. Do you remember what they were? The most important gift, of course, was the one God gave you when He gave you Jesus. But what kind of a gift was He? Was He a gift like my money clip, interesting but soon set aside and forgotten? Or was he like my necktie? Nice to have around every now and then but not really needed. Or was He like my wallet? Needed every day so much so that you couldn't get along without Him? He is where your identification is found.

Is Jesus the most precious gift that you've ever received? I'll ask the same question after Christmas a year from now. I'll be anxious to hear how you answer it.

Visual Aids:

Book with blank pages

NEW YEAR

Guess what, Jeremiah? this week we are getting launched into a brand new year. We'll be going where no one has ever been. It is exciting and maybe a little scary because we have no idea what tomorrow may bring.

To help us enter this new year I brought with me today a brand new book. It is really a nice book, isn't it? {hold up book} I think you are going to be surprised when I show you what is inside. See. There is nothing in it. No pictures, no numbers, no words, nothing. Page after page of blank pages. I can fill up the pages however I like. I can draw pictures, write stories, or add and subtract numbers. I can do something really nice or I can mess it up.

God has given us a gift something like this blank book. He has offered us, all of us, children and adults, a fresh start, a totally new year. Do you recall that we also had a book like this last year? We had many experiences that we could have written about in our journal. There were many good pages but we also had pages that we wish we had not written. Perhaps too many wasted pages or pages we now regret. However, yesterday is gone forever and we cannot go back and erase anything. The good news is that God has opened the door to the future for us, a future filled with opportunities for us to do good.

God's word announces: "Behold, I make all things new." He has forgiven us all our sins, cleansed us and given us blank pages that we can fill with beautiful stories.

We thank God for this great and open door with fresh, new beginnings and pray that we will be the boys and girls, men and women that we know He wants us to be.

It is like getting a new clean book to write our life's story in. We pray that when our last chapter is written God will smile and declare, "Well done, good and faithful servant."

Visual Aids:

Hatchet, artificial tree

GEORGE WASHINGTON

Jeremiah, today we are going to discuss the father of our country, our first president. His name was George Washington. There is a legend from his childhood that helps us to understand why he was such a good president.

When he was a small boy he saw some woodsmen chopping down trees in a nearby forest. He watched with fascination and excitement as sharp axes felled tall trees. When he got home he asked his father if he could have a little axe, sometimes called a hatchet. His father agreed to give him one but only after he had demonstrated how to safely handle it.

George was delighted. Outside he went and soon chopped up some little sticks to use as kindling to help start a fire in the fireplace. He also used his sharp hatchet to shape some tent pegs.

After awhile he went roaming around the backyard looking for something else to do with his hatchet when he came across a sturdy cherry tree. He had no permission to chop down trees but he thought, "I wonder if my hatchet is strong enough to cut down a live tree?" No one was looking so he gave his hatchet a mighty swing. {use back side of hatchet to knock over tree} With a crash the cherry tree came down. Oh, no, now he knew he was in big trouble. He quickly picked up his hatchet and ran away.

Later that day his father found the tree lying on its side. "George, I am so sad. Someone chopped down my favorite cherry tree. Do you know who may have done this?"

George, with his head bowed, quietly confessed, "Father, I cannot tell a lie. I did it." We can imagine that his father was very upset by what happened but pleased that his son had not lied to him but had spoken the truth.

As George grew older his reputation as a trustworthy and honest man continued to grow. He became known throughout the country as a righteous man who could be counted on to tell the truth.

Years later when this brand new country was preparing to choose the man who would be America's first president they declared "We want a leader who is wise and honest. Where can we find such a person?" Many citizens answered that question by pointing to George Washington. Here was a man who was honest and wise. He was the perfect choice to be our first president.

George's nephew, whose name was also George, later said of his uncle, "He began each day in prayer on his knees with his Bible open." What a marvelous example for all of us. That is where he received his strength and courage to be such a great leader during some very difficult times.

Visual Aids:
Heart-shaped
valentine card, cross

VALENTINE'S DAY

Jeremiah, it is Valentine's Day this week and I have a special valentine for you. It says, "I love you, Jeremiah. Will you be my valentine?" You're smiling just as I thought you would. I was quite sure that a card like this would make you happy. All of us delight in knowing that someone loves us.

Did you ever wonder how Valentine's Day got started? I did and I soon discovered that there are several versions of its origin. However, there is one that to me appears to be the most likely.

Years ago a Roman Emperor, Claudius, outlawed marriages because he feared his soldiers would not go to war if they had wives. However, one of his bishops, Pastor Valentine, refused to obey such foolish orders and continued to officiate at weddings. He knew it was wrong to outlaw love and marriage. As a result of his disobedience to the emperor, he was put in prison and sentenced to death. While in prison he fell in love with the jailer's daughter. He sent her a heart-shaped letter, confessed his love for her and signed it, "Your Valentine."

So a valentine became a symbol of our love for someone.

We know that God loves us very much and sent us a real valentine when He sent us Jesus. Jesus is absolute evidence of how much He loves us.

We use the cross as the symbol-a sign that can be seen- of how much we are loved. So you can see how the cross is like a valentine from God and is a constant reminder of the price that was paid by Jesus to prove His love for each one of the precious children.

PRETENDING YOU'RE SOMEONE ELSE

Friends, it was Halloween this week and it was lots of fun, wasn't it? Many boys and girls (and some adults, too) put on a mask or costume for a little while and pretended they were someone or something else.

We had so many interesting characters visit our house. There were children in animal costumes, space suits, clowns, super heroes, kings, queens, ghosts, and so many others. Each trick or treater received from us a healthy hunk of broccoli. {pause} I'm just kidding. Everyone was given a tasty treat.

Halloween is over but something strange has happened to Jeremiah. He is still wearing his Halloween mask. He has been wearing it for two days. He even wears it when he eats and when he goes to bed. He insisted on wearing it to chapel today. I've tried to explain to him that it is no longer Halloween and he should remove his mask but he doesn't want to do it.

Jeremiah, please, I'll ask you one more time, "Why won't you take off your mask?" Just whisper the answer to me, OK? {Jeremiah whispers in my ear} You are embarrassed to answer my question? Now I am really concerned. Please tell me what is going on. {Jeremiah again whispers} Oh, you think you would have more friends and people would like you better if you were someone else? Oh, that is not true. You are so very special just the way you are. I'm sure that's true but here is what I am going to do. I will slowly remove your mask and if your friends clap and cheer you will know that you never have to wear a mask or pretend you're someone else. I'm sure, Jeremiah, they love you best just the way you are. Your mask is coming off...{remove mask}

Jeremiah, I told you they loved you best just as you are. Look at the smiles and listen to the cheers.

Boys and girls, as much fun as it is to wear a mask and pretend that we are someone else for a little while, the best part of you is the part that is real. How you look, how you talk, how you act, and how you love is what makes you so very special just as you are.

Visual Aid:

Trick candles

EASTER LIGHT

Jeremiah, do you remember when we read in the Bible that Jesus said He was the light of the world? The apostle John adds that all the darkness in the world could not snuff out the light.

However, we know from the Scriptures that there were those who loved darkness and hated the light. Why? Because they could do evil deeds in the darkness and not be seen.

So when Jesus, the light of the world, came {light candles} they were furious. They no longer could hide what they were doing. Something had to change but they weren't about to change their evil ways. They got together and plotted how they could get rid of the light. Do you remember what they did next? They lied about Jesus, betrayed Him, whipped Him, mocked Him, put a crown of thorns on His head, spit on Him, crucified Him, nailed Him to a cross, and put Him to death. They were satisfied. Once and for all they had put out the light. {blow out candles and look away from the candles but keep talking} So they went off by themselves bragging about their ugly victory. The light was out, gone, extinguished, never to shine again. They laughed an evil laugh: ha, ha, ha. {keep talking until candles relight themselves; the children will see this and start cheering}

Look! Everybody, look! The light is shining again. They couldn't put it out. Jesus is alive! Life is stronger than death. Good wins over evil. Love has defeated hate. Yes! Yes! Oh yes!

Jesus lives. The light of the world continues to shine and its radiant splendor will end darkness forever. From the light of Jesus we received power to be his reflectors, letting our light shine everyday, everywhere, all around the world. Let it shine. Let it shine. Let it shine.

Let us sing together "This Little Light of Mine."

> "This little light of mine,
> I'm gonna let it shine.
> This little light of mine,
> I'm gonna let it shine.
> Let it shine, let it shine, let it shine.
>
> Hide it under a bushel? No!
> I'm gonna let it shine.
> Hide it under a bushel? No!
> I'm gonna let it shine.
> Let it shine, let it shine, let it shine.
>
> Don't let Satan blow it out,
> I'm gonna let it shine.
> Don't let Satan blow it out,
> I'm gonna let it shine.
> Let it shine, let it shine, let it shine
>
> Shine all over San Diego,
> I'm gonna let it shine.
> Shine all over San Diego,
> I'm gonna let it shine.
> Let it shine, let it shine, let it shine.
> (author unknown)

Visual aids:

Pictures of:

caterpillar, cocoon, butterfly

EASTER PARABLE

Jeremiah, it was a year ago that I visited Latvia. This is a tiny country that borders Russia. It is a long way from here. Very few people there speak our language so I had an interpreter with me who would repeat what I said in a language they understood.

I was telling them the story of the caterpillar and the butterfly when we encountered a problem. The interpreter could think of no word for caterpillar in the Latvian language. I quickly and quietly summarized for him the story. He smiled and then described the caterpillar as "a worm with a future." I thought that was a terrific description.

Here is the story that I told about "a worm with a future." It is an Easter parable.

Life for the caterpillar can be quite difficult. Each day is a struggle to find food. Some days they go to bed hungry because they found nothing to eat. Other days are happier because a delicious peach leaf served as a fine lunch. For the most part, however, life was not easy living down in the dust and dirt of the earth with each day a battle to survive.

One day a family of caterpillars noticed that a family member was really slowing down. Eventually he was hardly moving at all and they were quite concerned. They hoped that tomorrow would be a better day.

The next day they were all up early to check on their friend. To their horror, he wasn't moving at all. Nothing remained but an empty shell. {cocoon} They were convinced that something terrible had happened to him. They gathered around the empty shell and shed tears. Big caterpillar tears were flowing down their cheeks. Grief-stricken, with their heads bowed low, they continued to sob.

Oh, how sad were those foolish caterpillars. They should have looked up. Had they done so they would have seen high above them, soaring joyfully and free, their loved one now transformed into a beautiful butterfly {butterfly} celebrating a life so much better than they could ever imagine. Those pathetic caterpillars never looked up and continued to wail and mourn.

This story is a powerful parable of Easter. When Jesus was crucified, put to death, and his body placed in a tomb, it seemed like there was nothing left but an empty shell. His disciples were all crying and filled with despair.

On Easter morning the greatest news ever heard was announced by the angels, "He is risen!" He had conquered death and now had a glorious new body, one that would never die and soon would be on the road to heaven.

The good news is that all followers of Jesus share in His victory. Death for us will mean being transformed into a new life more wonderful than anything we could ever imagine.

Is it any wonder that the butterfly has become the symbol of Easter, a reminder of the resurrection victory with the assurance that for all God's children the best is yet to be?

May all of us remember this story every time we see a butterfly.